Summary

Cybersecurity vulnerabilities challenge governments, businesses, and individuals worldwide. Attacks have been initiated by individuals, as well as countries. Targets have included government networks, military defenses, companies, or political organizations, depending upon whether the attacker was seeking military intelligence, conducting diplomatic or industrial espionage, or intimidating political activists. In addition, national borders mean little or nothing to cyberattackers, and attributing an attack to a specific location can be difficult, which also makes a response problematic.

Congress has been actively involved in cybersecurity issues, holding hearings every year since 2001. There is no shortage of data on this topic: government agencies, academic institutions, think tanks, security consultants, and trade associations have issued hundreds of reports, studies, analyses, and statistics.

This report provides links to selected authoritative resources related to cybersecurity issues. This report includes information on

- "Legislation"
- "Hearings in the 112th Congress"
- "Executive Orders and Presidential Directives"
- "Data and Statistics"
- "Cybersecurity Glossaries"
- "Reports by Topic"
  - Government Accountability Office (GAO) reports
  - White House/Office of Management and Budget reports
  - Military/DOD
  - Cloud Computing
  - Critical Infrastructure
  - National Strategy for Trusted Identities in Cyberspace (NSTIC)
  - Cybercrime/Cyberwar
  - International
  - Education/Training/Workforce
  - Research and Development (R&D)
- "Related Resources: Other Websites"

The report will be updated as needed.

Contents

Tables

Contacts

Introduction

Cybersecurity is a sprawling topic that includes national, international, government, and private industry dimensions. More than 40 bills and resolutions with provisions related to cybersecurity have been introduced in the first session of the 112th Congress, including several proposing revisions to current laws. In the 111th Congress, the total was more than 60. Several of those bills received committee or floor action, but none have become law. In fact, no comprehensive cybersecurity legislation has been enacted since 2002.

This report provides links to cybersecurity hearings and legislation under consideration in the 112th Congress, as well as executive orders and presidential directives, data and statistics, glossaries, and authoritative reports.

For CRS analysis, please see the collection of CRS reports found on the Issues in Focus: Cybersecurity site.

Legislation

No major legislative provisions relating to cybersecurity have been enacted since 2002, despite many recommendations made over the past decade. The Obama Administration sent Congress a package of legislative proposals in May 2011[1] to give the federal government new authority to ensure that corporations that own the assets most critical to the nation's security and economic prosperity are adequately addressing the risks posed by cybersecurity threats.

Cybersecurity legislation is advancing in both chambers in the 112th Congress. The House introduced a series of bills that address a variety of issues—from toughening law enforcement of cybercrimes to giving the Department of Homeland Security oversight of federal information technology and critical infrastructure security to lessening liability for private companies that adopt cybersecurity best practices. The Senate is pursuing a comprehensive cybersecurity bill with several committees working to create a single vehicle for passage.

Table 1 and **Table 2** provide lists of major Senate and House legislation under current consideration in the 112th Congress, in order by date introduced. When viewed in HTML, the bill numbers are active links to the Bill Summary and Status page in the Legislative Information Service (LIS). The tables include bills with committee action, floor action, or significant legislative interest.

---

[1] White House, *International Strategy for Cyberspace Prosperity, Security, and Openness in a Networked World*, May 2011, at http://www.whitehouse.gov/sites/default/files/rss_viewer/international_strategy_for_cyberspace.pdf.

Table 1. Major Legislation: Senate (112th Congress)

Bill No.	Title	Committee(s)	Date Introduced
S. 413	Cybersecurity and Internet Freedom Act of 2011	Homeland Security and Governmental Affairs	February 17, 2011
S. 1151	Personal Data Privacy and Security Act of 2011	Judiciary	June 7, 2011
S. 1342	Grid Cyber Security Act	Energy and Natural Resources	July 11, 2011
S. 1535	Personal Data Protection and Breach Accountability Act of 2011	Judiciary	September 22, 2011
S. 2102	Cybersecurity Information Sharing Act of 2012	Homeland Security and Governmental Affairs	February 13, 2012
S. 2105	Cybersecurity Act of 2012	Homeland Security and Governmental Affairs	February 14, 2012
S. 2151	SECURE IT Act	Commerce, Science, and Transportation	March 1, 2012

Source: Legislative Information System (LIS).

Table 2. Major Legislation: House (112th Congress)

Bill No.	Title	Committee(s)	Date Introduced
H.R. 76	Cybersecurity Education Enhancement Act of 2011	Homeland Security; House Oversight and Government Reform	January 5, 2011
H.R. 174	Homeland Security Cyber and Physical Infrastructure Protection Act of 2011	Technology; Education and the Workforce; Homeland Security	January 5, 2011
H.R. 2096	Cybersecurity Enhancement Act of 2011	Science, Space, and Technology	June 2, 2011
H.R. 3523	Cyber Intel igence Sharing and Protection Act	Committee on Intelligence (Permanent Select)	November 30, 2011
H.R. 3674	PRECISE Act of 2011	Homeland Security; Oversight and Government Reform; Science, Space, and Technology; Judiciary; Intelligence (Permanent Select)	December 15, 2011
H.R. 4263	SECURE IT Act of 2012 Strengthening and Enhancing Cybersecurity by Using Research, Education, Information, and	Oversight and Government Reform, the Judiciary, Armed Services, and Intel igence (Permanent Select)	March 27, 2012
H.R. 3834	Advancing America's Networking and Information Technology Research and Development Act of 2012	Science, Space, and Technology	January 27, 2012
H.R. 4257	Federal Information Security Amendments Act of 2012	Oversight and Government Reform	April 18, 2012

Source: Legislative Information System (LIS).

Hearings in the 112th Congress

The following tables list cybersecurity hearings in the 112th Congress. **Table 3** and **Table 4** contain identical content but organized differently. **Table 3** lists House hearings arranged by date (most recent first), and **Table 4** lists House hearings arranged by committee. **Table 5** lists House markups by date; **Table 6** and **Table 7** contain identical content. **Table 6** lists Senate hearings arranged by date, and **Table 7** lists Senate hearings arranged by committee. When viewed in HTML, the document titles are active links.

Table 3. House Hearings (112th Congress), by Date

Title	Date	Committee	Subcommittee
Cyber Threats to Capital Markets and Corporate Accounts	June 1, 2012	Financial Services	Capital Markets and Government Sponsored Enterprises
Iranian Cyber Threat to U.S. Homeland	April 26, 2012	Homeland Security	Cybersecurity, Infrastructure Protection and Security Technologies and Counterterrorism and Intelligence
America is Under Cyber Attack: Why Urgent Action is Needed	April 24, 2012	Homeland Security	Oversight, Investigations and Management
The DHS and DOE National Labs: Finding Efficiencies and Optimizing Outputs in Homeland Security Research and Development	April 19, 2012	Homeland Security	Cybersecurity, Infrastructure Protection and Security Technologies
Cybersecurity: Threats to Communications Networks and Public-Sector Responses	March 28, 2012	Energy and Commerce	Communications and Technology
IT Supply Chain Security: Review of Government and Industry Efforts	March 27, 2012	Energy and Commerce	Oversight and Investigations
Fiscal 2013 Defense Authorization: IT and Cyber Operations	March 20, 2012	Armed Services	Emerging Threats and Capabilities
Cybersecurity: The Pivotal Role of Communications Networks	March 7, 2012	Energy and Commerce	Communications and Technology
NASA Cybersecurity: An Examination of the Agency's Information Security	February 29, 2012	Science, Space, and Technology	Investigations and Oversight
Critical Infrastructure Cybersecurity: Assessments of Smart Grid Security	February 28, 2012	Energy and Commerce	Oversight and Investigations
Hearing on Draft Legislative Proposal on Cybersecurity	December 6, 2011	Homeland Security	Cybersecurity, Infrastructure Protection and Security Technologies
Cyber Security: Protecting Your Small Business	December 1, 2011	Small Business	Healthcare and Technology
Cyber Security: Protecting Your Small Business	November 30, 2011	Small Business	Healthcare and Technology
Combating Online Piracy (H.R. 3261, Stop the Online Piracy Act)	November 16, 2011	Judiciary	
Cybersecurity: Protecting America's New Frontier	November 15, 2011	Judiciary	Crime, Terrorism and Homeland Security
Institutionalizing Irregular Warfare Capabilities	November 3, 2011	Armed Services	Emerging Threats and Capabilities

Title	Date	Committee	Subcommittee
Cloud Computing: What are the Security Implications?	October 6, 2011	Homeland Security	Cybersecurity, Infrastructure Protection and Security Technologies
Cyber Threats and Ongoing Efforts to Protect the Nation	October 4, 2011	Permanent Select Intelligence	
The Cloud Computing Outlook	September 21, 2011	Science, Space, and Technology	Technology and Innovation
Combating Cybercriminals	September 14, 2011	Financial Services	Financial Institutions and Consumer Credit
Cybersecurity: An Overview of Risks to Critical Infrastructure	July 26, 2011	Energy and Commerce	Oversight and Investigations
Cybersecurity: Assessing the Nation's Ability to Address the Growing Cyber Threat	July 7, 2011	Oversight and Government Reform	
Field Hearing: Hacked Off: Helping Law Enforcement Protect Private Financial Information	June 29, 2011	Financial Services (field hearing in Hoover, AL)	
Examining the Homeland Security Impact of the Obama Administration's Cybersecurity Proposal	June 24, 2011	Homeland Security	Cybersecurity, Infrastructure Protection and Security Technologies
Sony and Epsilon: Lessons for Data Security Legislation	June 2, 2011	Energy and Commerce	Commerce, Manufacturing, and Trade
Protecting the Electric Grid: the Grid Reliability and Infrastructure Defense Act	May 31, 2011	Energy and Commerce	
Unlocking the SAFETY Act's [Support Anti-terrorism by Fostering Effective Technologies - P.L. 107-296] Potential to Promote Technology and Combat Terrorism	May 26, 2011	Homeland Security	Cybersecurity, Infrastructure Protection, and Security Technologies
Protecting Information in the Digital Age: Federal Cybersecurity Research and Development Efforts	May 25, 2011	Science, Space and Technology	Research and Science Education
Cybersecurity: Innovative Solutions to Challenging Problems	May 25, 2011	Judiciary	Intellectual Property, Competition and the Internet
Cybersecurity: Assessing the Immediate Threat to the United States	May 25, 2011	Oversight and Government Reform	National Security, Homeland Defense and Foreign Operations
DHS Cybersecurity Mission: Promoting Innovation and Securing Critical Infrastructure	April 15, 2011	Homeland Security	Cybersecurity, Infrastructure Protection and Security Technologies
Communist Chinese Cyber-Attacks, Cyber-Espionage and Theft of American Technology	April 15, 2011	Foreign Affairs	Oversight and Investigations
Budget Hearing - National Protection and Programs Directorate, Cybersecurity and Infrastructure Protection Programs	March 31, 2011	Appropriations (closed/classified)	Energy and Power

Title	Date	Committee	Subcommittee
Examining the Cyber Threat to Critical Infrastructure and the American Economy	March 16, 2011	Homeland Security	Cybersecurity, Infrastructure Protection and Security Technologies
2012 Budget Request from U.S. Cyber Command	March 16, 2011	Armed Services	Emerging Threats and Capabilities
What Should the Department of Defense's Role in Cyber Be?	February 11, 2011	Armed Services	Emerging Threats and Capabilities
Preventing Chemical Terrorism: Building a Foundation of Security at Our Nation's Chemical Facilities	February 11, 2011	Homeland Security	Cybersecurity, Infrastructure Protection and Security Technologies
World Wide Threats	February 10, 2011	Permanent Select Intelligence	

Source: Compiled by the Congressional Research Service (CRS).

Table 4. House Hearings (112th Congress), by Committee

Committee	Subcommittee	Title	Date
Appropriations (closed/classified)		Budget Hearing - National Protection and Programs Directorate, Cybersecurity and Infrastructure Protection Programs	March 31, 2011
Armed Services	Emerging Threats and Capabilities	Fiscal 2013 Defense Authorization: IT and Cyber Operations	March 20, 2012
Armed Services	Emerging Threats and Capabilities	Institutionalizing Irregular Warfare Capabilities	November 3, 2011
Armed Services	Emerging Threats and Capabilities	2012 Budget Request for U.S. Cyber Command	March 16, 2011
Armed Services	Emerging Threats and Capabilities	What Should the Department of Defense's Role in Cyber Be?	February 11, 2011
Energy and Commerce	Communications and Technology	Cybersecurity: Threats to Communications Networks and Public-Sector Responses	March 28, 2012
Energy and Commerce	Oversight and Investigations	IT Supply Chain Security: Review of Government and Industry Efforts	March 27, 2012
Energy and Commerce	Communications and Technology	Cybersecurity: The Pivotal Role of Communications Networks	March 7, 2012
Energy and Commerce	Oversight and Investigations	Critical Infrastructure Cybersecurity: Assessments of Smart Grid Security	February 28, 2012
Energy and Commerce	Oversight and Investigations	Cybersecurity: An Overview of Risks to Critical Infrastructure	July 26, 2011
Energy and Commerce	Commerce, Manufacturing, and Trade	Sony and Epsilon: Lessons for Data Security Legislation	June 2, 2011
Energy and Commerce	Energy and Power	Protecting the Electric Grid: the Grid Reliability and Infrastructure Defense Act	May 31, 2011
Financial Services	Capital Markets and Government Sponsored Enterprises	Cyber Threats to Capital Markets and Corporate Account	June 1, 2012
Financial Services	Financial Institutions and Consumer Credit	Combating Cybercriminals	September 14, 2011
Financial Services	Field hearing in Hoover, AL	Field Hearing: "Hacked Off: Helping Law Enforcement Protect Private Financial Information	June 29, 2011
Foreign Affairs	Oversight and Investigations	Communist Chinese Cyber-Attacks, Cyber-Espionage and Theft of American Technology	April 15, 2011
Homeland Security	Cybersecurity, Infrastructure Protection and Security Technologies and Counterterrorism and Intelligence	Iranian Cyber Threat to U.S. Homeland	April 26, 2012
Homeland Security	Oversight, Investigations and Management	America is Under Cyber Attack: Why Urgent Action is Needed	April 24, 2012
Homeland Security	Cybersecurity, Infrastructure Protection and Security Technologies	The DHS and DOE National Labs: Finding Efficiencies and Optimizing Outputs in Homeland Security Research and Development	April 19, 2012
Homeland Security	Cybersecurity, Infrastructure Protection and Security Technologies	Hearing on Draft Legislative Proposal on Cybersecurity	December 6, 2011

Committee	Subcommittee	Title	Date
Homeland Security	Cybersecurity, Infrastructure Protection and Security Technologies	Cloud Computing: What are the Security Implications?	October 6, 2011
Homeland Security	Cybersecurity, Infrastructure Protection and Security Technologies	Examining the Homeland Security Impact of the Obama Administration's Cybersecurity Proposal	June 24, 2011
Homeland Security	Cybersecurity, Infrastructure Protection and Security Technologies	Unlocking the SAFETY Act's [Support Anti-terrorism by Fostering Effective Technologies - P.L. 107-296] Potential to Promote Technology and Combat Terrorism	May 26, 2011
Homeland Security	Cybersecurity, Infrastructure Protection and Security Technologies	DHS Cybersecurity Mission: Promoting Innovation and Securing Critical Infrastructure	April 15, 2011
Homeland Security	Cybersecurity, Infrastructure Protection and Security Technologies	Examining the Cyber Threat to Critical Infrastructure and the American Economy	March 16, 2011
Homeland Security	Cybersecurity, Infrastructure Protection and Security Technologies	Preventing Chemical Terrorism: Building a Foundation of Security at Our Nation's Chemical Facilities	February 11, 2011
Judiciary	Crime, Terrorism and Homeland Security	Combating Online Piracy (H.R. 3261, Stop the Online Piracy Act)	November 16, 2011
Judiciary	Crime, Terrorism and Homeland Security	Cybersecurity: Protecting America's New Frontier	November 15, 2011
Judiciary	Intellectual Property, Competition and the Internet	Cybersecurity: Innovative Solutions to Challenging Problems	May 25, 2011
Oversight and Government Reform		Cybersecurity: Assessing the Nation's Ability to Address the Growing Cyber Threat	July 7, 2011
Oversight and Government Reform	Subcommittee on National Security, Homeland Defense and Foreign Operations	Cybersecurity: Assessing the Immediate Threat to the United States	May 25, 2011
Permanent Select Intelligence		Cyber Threats and Ongoing Efforts to Protect the Nation	October 4, 2011
Permanent Select Intelligence		World Wide Threats	February 10, 2011
Science, Space and Technology	Investigations and Oversight	NASA Cybersecurity: An Examination of the Agency's Information Security	February 29, 2012
Science, Space and Technology	Technology and Innovation	The Cloud Computing Outlook	September 21, 2011
Science, Space and Technology	Research and Science Education	Protecting Information in the Digital Age: Federal Cybersecurity Research and Development Efforts	May 25, 2011
Small Business	Healthcare and Technology	Cyber Security: Protecting Your Small Business	November 30, 2011

Source: Compiled by CRS.

Table 5. House Markups (112ᵗʰ Congress), by Date

Title	Date	Committee	Subcommittee
Consideration and Markup of H.R. 3674	February 1, 2012	Homeland Security	Cybersecurity, Infrastructure Protection and Security Technologies
Markup: Draft Bill: Cyber Intelligence Sharing and Protection Act of 2011	December 1, 2011	Permanent Select Intelligence	
Markup on H.R. 2096, Cybersecurity Enhancement Act of 2011	July 21, 2011	Science, Space and Technology	
Discussion Draft of H.R. 2577, a bill to require greater protection for sensitive consumer data and timely notification in case of breach	June 15, 2011	Energy and Commerce	Commerce, Manufacturing, and Trade

Source: Compiled by CRS.

Table 6. Senate Hearings (112th Congress), by Date

Title	Date	Committee	Subcommittee
To receive testimony on U.S. Strategic Command and U.S. Cyber Command in review of the Defense Authorization Request for Fiscal Year 2013 and the Future Years Defense Program.	March 27, 2012	Armed Services	
To receive testimony on cybersecurity research and development in review of the Defense Authorization Request for Fiscal Year 2013 and the Future Years Defense Program	March 20, 2012	Armed Services	Emerging Threats and Capabilities
The Freedom of Information Act: Safeguarding Critical Infrastructure Information and the Public's Right to Know	March 13, 2012	Judiciary	
Securing America's Future: The Cybersecurity Act of 2012	February 16, 2012	Homeland Security and Governmental Affairs	
Cybercrime: Updating the Computer Fraud and Abuse Act to Protect Cyberspace and Combat Emerging Threats	September 7, 2011	Judiciary	
Role of Small Business in Strengthening Cybersecurity Efforts in the United States	July 25, 2011	Small Business and Entrepreneurship	
Privacy and Data Security: Protecting Consumers in the Modern World	June 29, 2011	Commerce, Science and Transportation	
Cybersecurity: Evaluating the Administration's Proposals	June 21, 2011	Judiciary	Crime and Terrorism
Cybersecurity and Data Protection in the Financial Sector	June 21, 2011	Banking, Housing and Urban Affairs	
Protecting Cyberspace: Assessing the White House Proposal	May 23, 2011	Homeland Security and Governmental Affairs	
Cybersecurity of the Bulk-Power System and Electric Infrastructure	May 5, 2011	Energy and Natural Resources	
To receive testimony on the health and status of the defense industrial base and its science and technology-related elements	May 3, 2011	Armed Services	Emerging Threats and Capabilities
Cyber Security: Responding to the Threat of Cyber Crime and Terrorism	April 12, 2011	Judiciary	Crime and Terrorism
Oversight of the Federal Bureau of Investigation	March 30, 2011	Judiciary	
Cybersecurity and Critical Electric Infrastructure[a]	March 15, 2011	Energy and Natural Resources	
Information Sharing in the Era of WikiLeaks: Balancing Security and Collaboration	March 10, 2011	Homeland Security and Governmental Affairs	
Homeland Security Department's Budget Submission for Fiscal Year 2012	February 17, 2011	Homeland Security and Governmental Affairs	

Source: Compiled by CRS.

a.   The March 15, 2011, hearing before the Committee on Energy and Natural Resources was closed. The hearing notice was removed from the committee's website.

Table 7. Senate Hearings (112th Congress), by Committee

Committee	Subcommittee	Title	Date
Armed Services	Emerging Threats and Capabilities	To receive testimony on cybersecurity research and development in review of the Defense Authorization Request for Fiscal Year 2013 and the Future Years Defense Program	March 30, 2012
Armed Services	Emerging Threats and Capabilities	To receive testimony on the health and status of the defense industrial base and its science and technology-related elements	May 3, 2011
Banking, Housing and Urban Affairs		Cybersecurity and Data Protection in the Financial Sector	June 21, 2011
Commerce, Science and Transportation		Privacy and Data Security: Protecting Consumers in the Modern World	June 29, 2011
Energy and Natural Resources		Cybersecurity of the Bulk-Power System and Electric Infrastructure	May 5, 2011
Energy and Natural Resources (closed)		Cybersecurity and Critical Electric Infrastructure[a]	March 15, 2011
Homeland Security & Governmental Affairs		Securing America's Future: The Cybersecurity Act of 2012	February 16, 2012
Homeland Security and Governmental Affairs		Protecting Cyberspace: Assessing the White House Proposal	May 23, 2011
Homeland Security and Governmental Affairs		Information Sharing in the Era of WikiLeaks: Balancing Security and Collaboration	March 10, 2011
Homeland Security and Governmental Affairs		Homeland Security Department's Budget Submission for Fiscal Year 2012	February 17, 2011
Judiciary		The Freedom of Information Act: Safeguarding Critical Infrastructure Information and the Public's Right to Know	March 13, 2012
Judiciary		Cybercrime: Updating the Computer Fraud and Abuse Act to Protect Cyberspace and Combat Emerging Threats	September 7, 2011
Judiciary	Crime and Terrorism	Cybersecurity: Evaluating the Administration's Proposals	June 21, 2011
Judiciary	Crime and Terrorism	Cyber Security: Responding to the Threat of Cyber Crime and Terrorism	April 12, 2011
Judiciary		Oversight of the Federal Bureau of Investigation	March 30, 2011
Small Business and Entrepreneurship		Role of Small Business in Strengthening Cybersecurity Efforts in the United States	July 25, 2011

Source: Compiled by CRS.

a. The March 15, 2011 hearing before the Committee on Energy and Natural Resources was closed. The hearing notice was removed from the committee's website.

Executive Orders and Presidential Directives

Executive orders are official documents through which the President of the United States manages the operations of the federal government. Presidential directives pertain to all aspects of U.S. national security policy and are signed or authorized by the President.

The following reports provide additional information on executive orders and presidential directives:

- CRS Report RS20846, *Executive Orders: Issuance, Modification, and Revocation*, by Vanessa K. Burrows and

- CRS Report 98-611, *Presidential Directives: Background and Overview*, by L. Elaine Halchin.

Table 8 provides a list of executive orders and presidential directives pertaining to information and computer security.

Table 8. Executive Orders and Presidential Directives

(by date of issuance)

Title	Date	Source	Notes
E.O. 13587, Structural Reforms to Improve the Security of Classified Networks and the Responsible http://www.gpo.gov/fdsys/pkg/FR-2011-10-13/pdf/2011-26729.pdf	October 7, 2011	White House	This order directs structural reforms to ensure responsible sharing and safeguarding of classified information on computer networks that shall be consistent with appropriate protections for privacy and civil liberties. Agencies bear the primary responsibility for meeting these twin goals. These policies and minimum standards will address all agencies that operate or access classified computer networks, all users of classified computer networks (including contractors and others who operate or access classified computer networks controlled by the Federal Government), and all classified information on those networks.
E.O. 13407, Public Alert and Warning System http://www.gpo.gov/fdsys/pkg/WCPD-2006-07-03/pdf/WCPD-2006-07-03-Pg1226.pdf	June 26, 2006	White House	Assigns the Secretary of Homeland Security the responsibility to establish or adopt, as appropriate, common alerting and warning protocols, standards, terminology, and operating procedures for the public alert and warning system to enable interoperability and the secure delivery of coordinated messages to the American people through as many communication pathways as practicable, taking account of Federal Communications Commission rules as provided by law.
HSPD-7, Homeland Security Presidential Directive No. 7: Critical Infrastructure Identification, Prioritization, and Protection http://www.dhs.gov/xabout/laws/gc_121459798952.shtm	December 17, 2003	White House	Assigns the Secretary of Homeland Security the responsibility of coordinating the nation's overall efforts in critical infrastructure protection across all sectors. HSPD-7 also designates the Department of Homeland Security (DHS) as lead agency for the nation's information and telecommunications sectors.
E.O. 13286, Amendment of Executive Orders, and Other Actions, in Connection With the Transfer of Certain Functions to the Secretary of Homeland Security http://edocket.access.gpo.gov/2003/pdf/03-5343.pdf	February 28, 2003	White House	Designates the Secretary of Homeland Security the Executive Agent of the National Communication System Committee of Principals, which are the agencies, designated by the President, that own or lease telecommunication assets identified as part of the National Communication System, or which bear policy, regulatory, or enforcement responsibilities of importance to national security and emergency preparedness telecommunications.

Title	Date	Source	Notes
Presidential Decision Directive/NSC-63 http://www.fas.org/irp/offdocs/pdd/pdd-63.htm	May 22, 1998	White House	Sets as a national goal the ability to protect the nation's critical infrastructure from intentional attacks (both physical and cyber) by the year 2003. According to the PDD, any interruptions in the ability of these infrastructures to provide their goods and services must be "brief, infrequent, manageable, geographically isolated, and minimally detrimental to the welfare of the United States."
NSD-42, National Security Directive 42 - National Policy for the Security of National Security Telecommunications and Information Systems http://bushlibrary.tamu.edu/research/pdfs/nsd/nsd42.pdf	July 5, 1990	White House	Establishes the National Security Telecommunications and Information Systems Security Committee, now called the Committee on National Security Systems (CNSS). CNSS is an interagency committee, chaired by the Department of Defense. Among other assignments, NSD-42 directs the CNSS to provide system security guidance for national security systems to executive departments and agencies; and submit annually to the Executive Agent an evaluation of the security status of national security systems. NSD-42 also directs the Committee to interact, as necessary, with the National Communications System Committee of Principals.
E.O. 12472, Assignment of National Security and Emergency Preparedness Telecommunications Functions (amended by E.O. 13286 of February 28, 2003 and changes made by E.O. 13407, June 26, 2006) http://www.ncs.gov/library/policy_docs/eo_12472.html	April 3, 1984	National Communications System (NCS)	Established a national communication system as those telecommunication assets owned or leased by the federal government that can meet the national security and emergency preparedness needs of the federal government, together with an administrative structure that could ensure that a national telecommunications infrastructure is developed that is responsive to national security and emergency preparedness needs.

Note: Descriptions compiled by CRS from government websites.

Data and Statistics

This section identifies data and statistics from government, industry, and IT security firms regarding the current state of cybersecurity threats in the United States and internationally. These include incident estimates, costs, and annual reports on data security breaches, identity theft, cyber crime, malware, and network security.

Table 9. Data and Statistics: Cyber Incidents, Data Breaches, Cyber Crime

Title	Date	Source	Pages	Notes
ICS-CERT Incident Response Summary Report http://www.us-cert.gov/control_systems/pdf/ICS-CERT_Incident_Response_Summary_Report_09_11.pdf	June 28, 2012	U.S. Industrial Control System Cyber Emergency Response Team (ICS-CERT)	17	The number of reported cyberattacks on U.S. critical infrastructure increased sharply—from 9 incidents in 2009 to 198 in 2011; water sector-specific incidents, when added to the incidents that affected several sectors, accounted for more than ha f of the incidents; in more than ha f of the most serious cases, implementing best practices such as login imitation or properly configured firewall, would have deterred the attack, reduced the time it would have taken to detect an attack, and minimize its impact.
Worldwide Threat Assessment: Infection Rates and Threat Trends by Location http://www.microsoft.com/security/sir/threat/default.aspx#!introduction	ongoing	Microsoft Security Intel igence Report (SIR)	N/A	Data on infection rates, malicious websites and threat trends by regional location, worldwide.
McAfee Research & Reports (multiple) http://www.mcafee.com/us/about/newsroom/research-reports.aspx	2009-2012	McAfee	N/A	Links to reports on cybersecurity threats, malware, cybercrime, and spam.
Significant Cyber Incidents Since 2006 http://csis.org/pub ication/cyber-events-2006	January 19, 2012	Center for Strategic and International Studies (CSIS)	9	A ist of significant cyber events since 2006. From the report, "Significance is in the eye of the beholder, but we focus on successful attacks on government agencies, defense and high tech companies, or economic crimes with losses of more than a million dollars."
2011 ITRC Breach Report Key Findings http://www.idtheftcenter.org/artman2/publish/headlines/Breaches_2011.shtml	December 10, 2011	Identity Theft Resource Center (ITRC)	N/A	According to the report, hacking attacks were responsible for more than one-quarter (25.8%) of the data breaches recorded in the Identity Theft Resource Center's *2011 Breach Report*, hitting a five-year all time high. This was followed by "Data on the Move" (when an electronic storage device, laptop or paper folders leave the office where it is normally stored) and "Insider Theft," at 18.1% and 13.4% respectively.

Title	Date	Source	Pages	Notes
The Risk of Social Engineering on Information Security: A Survey of IT Professionals http://www.checkpoint.com/press/downloads/social-engineering-survey.pdf	September 2011	Check Point	7	[The] report reveals 48% of large companies and 32% of companies of all sizes surveyed have been victims of social engineering, experiencing 25 or more attacks in the past two years, costing businesses anywhere from $25,000 to over $100,000 per security incident. [P]hishing and social networking tools are the most common sources of socially engineered threats.
Second Annual Cost of Cyber Crime Study http://www.arcsight.com/collateral/whitepapers/2011_Cost_of_Cyber_Crime_Study_August.pdf	August 2011	Ponemon Institute	30	[T]he median annualized cost for 50 benchmarked organizations is $5.9 million per year, with a range from $1.5 million to $36.5 mil ion each year per company. This represents an increase in median cost of 56% from [Ponemon's] first cyber cost study published last year.
Revealed: Operation Shady RAT: an Investigation of Targeted Intrusions into 70+ Global Companies, Governments, and Non-Profit Organizations During the Last 5 Years http://www.mcafee.com/us/resources/white-papers/wp-operation-shady-rat.pdf	August 2, 2011	McAfee Research Labs	14	A comprehensive analysis of victim profiles from a five-year targeted operation which penetrated 72 government and other organizations, most of them in the United States, and copied everything from military secrets to industrial designs. See page 4 for types of compromised parties, page 5 for geographic distribution of victim's country of origin, pages 7-9 for types of victims, and pages 10-13 for the number of intrusions for 2007-2010.
2010 Annual Study: U.S. Cost of a Data Breach http://www.symantec.com/content/en/us/about/media/pdfs/symantec_ponemon_data_breach_costs_report.pdf?om_ext_cid= biz_socmed_twitter_facebook_marketwire_linkedin_2011Mar_worldwide_costofdatabreach	March 2011	Ponemon Institute/Symantec	39	The average organizational cost of a data breach increased to $7.2 mil ion and cost companies an average of $214 per compromised record.
FY2010 Report to Congress on the Implementation of the Federal Information Security Management Act of 2002 http://www.whitehouse.gov/sites/default/files/omb/assets/egov_docs/FY10_FISMA.pdf	March 2011	White House/ Office of Management and Budget	48	The number of attacks against federal networks increased nearly 40% last year, while the number of incidents targeting U.S. computers overall was down roughly 1% for the same period. (See pp. 12-13).

Title	Date	Source	Pages	Notes
A Good Decade for Cybercrime: McAfee's Look Back at Ten Years of Cybercrime http://www.mcafee.com/us/resources/reports/rp-good-decade-for-cybercrime.pdf	December 29, 2010	McAfee	11	A review of the most publicized, pervasive, and costly cybercrime exploits from 2000-2010.

Note: Statistics are from the source publication and have not been independently verified by CRS.

Cybersecurity Glossaries

Table 10 includes links to glossaries of useful cybersecurity terms, including those related to cloud computing and cyberwarfare.

Table 10. Glossaries of Cybersecurity Terms

Title	Source	Date	Pages	Notes
Cloud Computing Reference Architecture http://collaborate.nist.gov/twiki-cloud-computing/pub/CloudComputing/ReferenceArchitectureTaxonomy/NIST_SP_500-292_-_090611.pdf	National Institute of Standards and Technology (NIST)	September 2011	35	Provides guidance to specific communities of practitioners and researchers.
Glossary of Key Information Security Terms http://collaborate.nist.gov/twiki-cloud-computing/pub/CloudComputing/ReferenceArchitectureTaxonomy/NIST_SP_500-292_-_090611.pdf	NIST	February 2011	211	The glossary provides a central resource of terms and definitions most commonly used in NIST information security publications and in Committee for National Security Systems (CNSS) information assurance publications.
CIS Consensus Information Security Metrics http://collaborate.nist.gov/twiki-cloud-computing/pub/CloudComputing/ReferenceArchitectureTaxonomy/NIST_SP_500-292_-_090611.pdf	Center for Internet Security	November 2010	175	Provides definitions for security professionals to measure some of the most important aspects of the information security status. The goal is to give an organization the ability to repeatedly evaluate security in a standardized way, allowing it to identify trends, understand the impact of activities and make responses to improve the security status. (Free registration required.)
Joint Terminology for Cyberspace Operations http://collaborate.nist.gov/twiki-cloud-computing/pub/CloudComputing/ReferenceArchitectureTaxonomy/NIST_SP_500-292_-_090611.pdf	Chairman of the Joint Chiefs of Staff	November 1, 2010	16	This lexicon is the starting point for normalizing terms in all cyber-related documents, instructions, CONOPS, and publications as they come up for review.

Title	Source	Date	Pages	Notes
Department of Defense Dictionary of Military and Associated Terms http://collaborate.nist.gov/twiki-cloud-computing/pub/CloudComputing/ReferenceArchitectureTaxonomy/NIST_SP_500-292_-_090611.pdf	Chairman of the Joint Chiefs of Staff	November 8, 2010 (as amended through January 15, 2012)	547	Provides joint policy and guidance for Information Assurance (IA) and Computer Network Operations (CNO) activities.
DHS Risk Lexicon http://www.dhs.gov/x ibrary/assets/dhs-risk-lexicon-2010.pdf	Department of Homeland Security (DHS) Risk Steering Committee	September 2010	72	The lexicon promulgates a common language, faci itates the clear exchange of structured and unstructured data, and provides consistency and clear understanding with regard to the usage of terms by the risk community across the DHS.

Note: Highlights compiled by CRS from the reports.

Reports by Topic

This section gives references to analytical reports on cybersecurity from CRS, other governmental agencies, and trade organizations. The reports are grouped under the following cybersecurity topics: policy framework overview, critical infrastructure, and cybercrime and national security.

For each topic, CRS reports are listed first and then followed by tables with reports from other organizations. The overview reports provide an analysis of a broad range of cybersecurity issues (**Table 11** to **Table 16**). The critical infrastructure reports (**Table 17**) analyze cybersecurity issues related to telecom infrastructure, the electricity grid, and industrial control systems. The cybercrime and national security reports (**Table 18**) analyze a wide range of cybersecurity issues, including identify theft and government policies for dealing with cyberwar scenarios. In addition, tables with selected reports on international efforts to address cybersecurity problems, training for cybersecurity professionals, and research and development efforts in other areas are also provided (**Table 19** to **Table 21**).

CRS Reports Overview: Cybersecurity Policy Framework

- CRS Report R42114, *Federal Laws Relating to Cybersecurity: Discussion of Proposed Revisions*, by Eric A. Fischer

- CRS Report R41941, *The Obama Administration's Cybersecurity Proposal: Criminal Provisions*, by Gina Stevens

- CRS Report R40150, *A Federal Chief Technology Officer in the Obama Administration: Options and Issues for Consideration*, by John F. Sargent Jr.

- CRS Report R42409, *Cybersecurity: Selected Legal Issues*, by Edward C. Liu et al.

Table 11. Selected Reports: Cybersecurity Overview

Title	Source	Date	Pages	Notes
Cyber-security: The Vexed Question of Global Rules: An Independent Report on Cyber-Preparedness Around the World http://www.dhs.gov/xlibrary/assets/dhs-risk-lexicon-2010.pdf	McAfee and the Security Defense Agenda	February 2012	108	The report examines the current state of cyber-preparedness around the world, and is based on survey results from 80 policy-makers and cybersecurity experts in the government, business, and academic sectors from 27 countries. The countries were ranked on their state of cyber-preparedness.
Mission Critical: A Public-Private Strategy for Effective Cybersecurity http://businessroundtable.org/uploads/studies-reports/downloads/2011_10_Mission_Critical_A_Public-Private_Strategy_for_Effective_Cybersecurity_4_20_12.pdf	Business Roundtable	October 11, 2011	28	According to the report, "[p]ub ic policy solutions must recognize the absolute importance of leveraging po icy foundations that support effective global risk management, in contrast to "check-the-box" compliance approaches that can undermine security and cooperation. The document concludes with specific policy proposals and activity commitments.
World Cybersecurity Technology Research Summit (Be fast 2011) http://www.csit.qub.ac.uk/media/pdf/Filetoupload,252359,en.pdf	Centre for Secure Information Technologies (CSIT)	September 12, 2011	14	The Belfast 2011 event attracted international cyber security experts from leading research institutes, government bodies, and industry who gathered to discuss current cyber security threats, predict future threats and the necessary mitigation techniques, and to develop a collective strategy for next research.
A Review of Frequently Used Cyber Analogies http://www.nsci-va.org/WhitePapers/2011-07-22-Cyber Analogies Whitepaper-K McKee.pdf	National Security Cyberspace Institute	July 22, 2011	7	The current cybersecurity crisis can be described several ways with numerous metaphors. Many compare the current crisis with the lawlessness to that of the Wild West and the out-dated tactics and race to security with the Cold War. When treated as a distressed ecosystem, the work of both national and international agencies to eradicate many infectious diseases serves as a model as how poor health can be corrected with proper resources and execution. Before these issues are discussed, what cyberspace actually is must be identified.
America's Cyber Future: Security and Prosperity in the Information Age http://www.cnas.org/node/6405	Center for a New American Security	June 1, 2011	296	To help U.S. policymakers address the growing danger of cyber insecurity, this two-volume report features chapters on cyber security strategy, policy, and technology by some of the world's leading experts on international relations, national security, and information technology.

Title	Source	Date	Pages	Notes
Resilience of the Internet Interconnection Ecosystem http://www.enisa.europa.eu/act/res/other-areas/inter-x/report/interx-report	European Network and Information Security Agency (ENISA)	April 11, 2011	238	Part I: Summary and Recommendations; Part II: State of the Art Review (a detailed description of the Internet's routing mechanisms and analysis of their robustness at the technical, economic and po icy levels.); Part III: Report on the Consultation (a broad range of stakeholders were consulted. This part reports on the consultation and summarizes the results). Part IV: Bib iography and Appendices.
Improving our Nation's Cybersecurity through the Public-Private Partnership: a White Paper http://www.cdt.org/files/pdfs/20110308_cbyersec_paper.pdf	Business Software Alliance, Center for Democracy & Technology, U.S. Chamber of Commerce, Internet Security Alliance, Tech America	March 8, 2011	26	This paper proposes expanding the existing partnership within the framework of the National Infrastructure Protection Plan. Specifically, it makes a series of recommendations that build upon the conclusions of President Obama's *Cyberspace Policy Review*.
Cybersecurity Two Years Later http://csis.org/files/publication/110128_Lewis_CybersecurityTwoYearsLater_Web.pdf	CSIS Commission on Cybersecurity for the 44th Presidency, Center for Strategic and International Studies	January 2011	22	From the report: "We thought then [in 2008] that securing cyberspace had become a critical challenge for national security, which our nation was not prepared to meet.... In our view, we are still not prepared."
Toward Better Usability, Security, and Privacy of Information Technology: Report of a Workshop http://www.nap.edu/catalog.php?record_id=12998	National Research Council	September 21, 2010	70	Discusses computer system security and privacy, their relationship to usability, and research at their intersection. This is drawn from remarks made at the National Research Council's July 2009 *Workshop on Usability, Security and Privacy of Computer Systems* as well as recent reports from the NRC's Computer Science and Telecommunications Board on security and privacy.
National Security Threats in Cyberspace http://nationalstrategy.com/Portals/0/documents/National%20Security%20Threats%20in%20Cyberspace.pdf	Joint Workshop of the National Security Threats in Cyberspace and the National Strategy Forum	September 15, 2009	37	The two-day workshop brought together more than two dozen experts with diverse backgrounds: physicists; telecommunications executives; Si icon Valley entrepreneurs; federal law enforcement, military, homeland security, and intelligence officials; congressional staffers; and civil liberties advocates. For two days they engaged in an open-ended discussion of cyber policy as it relates to national security, under Chatham House Rules: their comments were for the pub ic record, but they were not for attribution.

Note: Highlights compiled by CRS from the reports.

Table 12. Selected Government Reports: Government Accountability Office (GAO)

Title	Date	Pages	Notes
Information Security: Cyber Threats Facilitate Ability to Commit Economic Espionage http://www.gao.gov/products/GAO-12-876T	June 28, 2012	20	This statement discusses (1) cyber threats facing the nation's systems, (2) reported cyber incidents and their impacts, (3) security controls and other techniques available for reducing risk, and (4) the responsibilities of key federal entities in support of protecting IP.
Cybersecurity: Challenges to Securing the Modernized Electricity Grid http://www.gao.gov/products/GAO-12-507T	February 28, 2012	19	As GAO reported in January 2011, securing smart grid systems and networks presented a number of key challenges that required attention by government and industry. GAO made several recommendations to the Federal Energy Regulatory Commission (FERC) aimed at addressing these challenges. The commission agreed with these recommendations and described steps it is taking to implement them.
Critical Infrastructure Protection: Cybersecurity Guidance Is Available, but More Can Be Done to Promote Its Use http://www.gao.gov/products/GAO-12-92	December 9, 2011	77	Given the plethora of guidance available, individual entities within the sectors may be challenged in identifying the guidance that is most applicable and effective in improving their security posture. Improved knowledge of the guidance that is available could help both federal and private sector decision makers better coordinate their efforts to protect critical cyber-reliant assets.
Cybersecurity Human Capital: Initiatives Need Better Planning and Coordination http://www.gao.gov/products/GAO-12-8	November 29, 2011	86	All the agencies GAO reviewed faced challenges determining the size of their cybersecurity workforce because of variations in how work is defined and the lack of an occupational series specific to cybersecurity. With respect to other workforce planning practices, all agencies had defined roles and responsibilities for their cybersecurity workforce, but these roles did not always align with guide ines issued by the federal Chief Information Officers Council and National Institute of Standards and Technology (NIST)
Federal Chief Information Officers: Opportunities Exist to Improve Role in Information Technology Management http://www.gao.gov/products/GAO-11-634	October 17, 2011	72	GAO is recommending that OMB update its guidance to establish measures of accountability for ensuring that CIOs' responsibilities are fully implemented and require agencies to establish internal processes for documenting lessons learned.
Information Security: Additional Guidance Needed to Address Cloud Computing Concerns http://www.gao.gov/products/GAO-12-130T	October 5, 2011	17	Twenty-two of 24 major federal agencies reported that they were either concerned or very concerned about the potential information security risks associated with cloud computing. GAO recommended that the NIST issue guidance specific to cloud computing security.
Information Security: Weaknesses Continue Amid New Federal Efforts to Implement Requirements http://www.gao.gov/products/GAO-12-137	October 3, 2011	49	Weaknesses in information security policies and practices at 24 major federal agencies continue to place the confidentiality, integrity, and availability of sensitive information and information systems at risk. Consistent with this risk, reports of security incidents from federal agencies are on the rise, increasing over 650% over the past 5 years. Each of the 24 agencies reviewed had weaknesses in information security controls.

Title	Date	Pages	Notes
Federal Chief Information Officers: Opportunities Exist to Improve Role in Information Technology Management http://www.gao.gov/products/GAO-11-634	October 17, 2011	72	GAO is recommending that the Office of Management and Budget (OMB) update its guidance to establish measures of accountability for ensuring that CIOs' responsibilities are fully implemented and require agencies to establish internal processes for documenting lessons learned.
Defense Department Cyber Efforts: Definitions, Focal Point, and Methodology Needed for DoD to Develop Full-Spectrum Cyberspace Budget Estimates http://www.gao.gov/products/GAO-11-695R	July 29, 2011	33	This letter discusses the Department of Defense's cyber and information assurance budget for fiscal year 2012 and future years defense spending. The objectives of this review were to (1) assess the extent to which DOD has prepared an overarching budget estimate for full-spectrum cyberspace operations across the department; and (2) identify the challenges DOD has faced in providing such estimates.
Continued Attention Needed to Protect Our Nation's Critical Infrastructure http://www.gao.gov/products/GAO-11-463T	July 26, 2011	20	A number of significant challenges remain to enhancing the security of cyber-reliant critical infrastructures, such as (1) implementing actions recommended by the president's cybersecurity policy review; (2) updating the national strategy for securing the information and communications infrastructure; (3) reassessing DHS's planning approach to critical infrastructure protection; (4) strengthening public-private partnerships, particularly for information sharing; (5) enhancing the national capability for cyber warning and analysis; (6) addressing global aspects of cybersecurity and governance; and (7) securing the modernized electricity grid.
Defense Department Cyber Efforts: DoD Faces Challenges in Its Cyber Activities http://www.gao.gov/products/GAO-11-75	July 25, 2011	79	GAO recommends that DOD evaluate how it is organized to address cybersecurity threats; assess the extent to which it has developed joint doctrine that addresses cyberspace operations; examine how it assigned command and control responsibilities; and determine how it identifies and acts to mitigate key capability gaps involving cyberspace operations.
Critical Infrastructure Protection: Key Private and Public Cyber Expectations Need to Be Consistently Addressed http://www.gao.gov/products/GAO-10-628	August 16, 2010	38	The Special Assistant to the President and Cybersecurity Coordinator and the Secretary of Homeland Security, should take two actions: (1) use the results of this report to focus their information-sharing efforts, including their relevant pilot projects, on the most desired services, including providing timely and actionable threat and alert information, access to sensitive or classified information, a secure mechanism for sharing information, and providing security clearance and (2) bolster the efforts to build out the National Cybersecurity and Communications Integration Center as the central focal point for leveraging and integrating the capabilities of the private sector, civilian government, law enforcement, the military, and the intelligence community.

Title	Date	Pages	Notes
Information Security: State Has Taken Steps to Implement a Continuous Monitoring Application, but Key Challenges Remain http://www.gao.gov/products/GAO-11-149	July 8, 2011	63	The Department of State implemented a custom application called iPost and a risk scoring program that is intended to provide continuous monitoring capabilities of information security risk to elements of its information technology (IT) infrastructure. To improve implementation of iPost at State, the Secretary of State should direct the Chief Information Officer to develop, document, and maintain an iPost configuration management and test process.
Cybersecurity: Continued Attention Needed to Protect Our Nation's Critical Infrastructure and Federal Information Systems http://www.gao.gov/products/GAO-11-463T	March 16, 2011	16	Executive branch agencies have made progress instituting several governmentwide initiatives that are aimed at bolstering aspects of federal cybersecurity, such as reducing the number of federal access points to the Internet, establishing security configurations for desktop computers, and enhancing situational awareness of cyber events. Despite these efforts, the federal government continues to face significant challenges in protecting the nation's cyber-reliant critical infrastructure and federal information systems.
Electricity Grid Modernization: Progress Being Made on Cybersecurity Guidelines, but Key Challenges Remain to be Addressed http://www.gao.gov/products/GAO-11-117	January 12, 2011	50	GAO identified the following six key challenges: (1) Aspects of the regulatory environment may make it difficult to ensure smart grid systems' cybersecurity. (2) Utilities are focusing on regulatory compliance instead of comprehensive security. (3) The electric industry does not have an effective mechanism for sharing information on cybersecurity. (4) Consumers are not adequately informed about the benefits, costs, and risks associated with smart grid systems. (5) There is a lack of security features being built into certain smart grid systems. (6) The electricity industry does not have metrics for evaluating cybersecurity.
Information Security: Federal Agencies Have Taken Steps to Secure Wireless Networks, but Further Actions Can Mitigate Risk http://www.gao.gov/products/GAO-11-43	November 30, 2010	50	Existing governmentwide guidelines and oversight efforts do not fully address agency implementation of leading wireless security practices. Until agencies take steps to better implement these leading practices, and OMB takes steps to improve governmentwide oversight, wireless networks will remain at an increased vulnerability to attack.
Cyberspace Policy: Executive Branch Is Making Progress Implementing 2009 Policy Review Recommendations, but Sustained Leadership Is Needed http://www.gao.gov/products/GAO-11-24	October 6, 2010	66	Of the 24 recommendations in the President's May 2009 cyber policy review report, 2 have been fully implemented, and 22 have been partially implemented. While these efforts appear to be steps forward, agencies were largely not able to provide milestones and plans that showed when and how implementation of the recommendations was to occur.
DHS Efforts to Assess and Promote Resiliency Are Evolving but Program Management Could Be Strengthened http://www.gao.gov/products/GAO-10-772	September 23, 2010	46	The Department of Homeland Security (DHS) has not developed an effective way to ensure that critical national infrastructure, such as electrical grids and telecommunications networks, can bounce back from a disaster. DHS has conducted surveys and vulnerability assessments of critical infrastructure to identify gaps, but has not developed a way to measure whether owners and operators of that infrastructure adopt measures to reduce risks.

Title	Date	Pages	Notes
Information Security: Progress Made on Harmonizing Policies and Guidance for National Security and Non-National Security Systems http://www.gao.gov/products/GAO-10-916	September 15, 2010	38	OMB and NIST estab ished policies and guidance for civi ian non-national security systems, while other organizations, including the Committee on National Security Systems (CNSS), DOD, and the U.S. intel igence community, have developed policies and guidance for national security systems. GAO was asked to assess the progress of federal efforts to harmonize po icies and guidance for these two types of systems
United States Faces Challenges in Addressing Global Cybersecurity and Governance http://www.gao.gov/products/GAO-10-606	August 2, 2010	53	GAO recommends that the Special Assistant to the President and Cybersecurity Coordinator should make recommendations to appropriate agencies and interagency coordination committees regarding any necessary changes to more effectively coordinate and forge a coherent national approach to cyberspace policy.
Federal Guidance Needed to Address Control Issues With Implementing Cloud Computing http://www.gao.gov/products/GAO-10-513	July 1, 2010	53	To assist federal agencies in identifying uses for cloud computing and information security measures to use in implementing cloud computing, the Director of OMB should establish milestones for completing a strategy for implementing the federal cloud computing initiative.
Continued Attention Is Needed to Protect Federal Information Systems from Evolving Threats http://www.gao.gov/products/GAO-10-834t	June 16, 2010	15	Multiple opportunities exist to improve federal cybersecurity. To address identified deficiencies in agencies' security controls and shortfalls in their information security programs, GAO and agency inspectors general have made hundreds of recommendations over the past several years, many of which agencies are implementing. In addition, the White House, the Office of Management and Budget, and certain federal agencies have undertaken several governmentwide initiatives intended to enhance information security at federal agencies. While progress has been made on these initiatives, they all face challenges that require sustained attention, and GAO has made several recommendations for improving the implementation and effectiveness of these initiatives.
Information Security: Concerted Response Needed to Resolve Persistent Weaknesses http://www.gao.gov/products/GAO-10-536t	March 24, 2010	21	Without proper safeguards, federal computer systems are vulnerable to intrusions by individuals who have malicious intentions and can obtain sensitive information. The need for a vigilant approach to information security has been demonstrated by the pervasive and sustained cyber attacks against the United States; these attacks continue to pose a potentially devastating impact to systems as well as the operations and critical infrastructures that they support.
Cybersecurity: Continued Attention Is Needed to Protect Federal Federal Information Systems from Evolving Threats http://www.gao.gov/products/GAO-11-463T	March 16, 2010	15	The White House, the Office of Management and Budget, and certain federal agencies have undertaken several governmentwide initiatives intended to enhance information security at federal agencies. While progress has been made on these initiatives, they all face challenges that require sustained attention, and GAO has made several recommendations for improving the implementation and effectiveness of these initiatives.

Cybersecurity: Authoritative Reports and Resources

Title	Date	Pages	Notes
Concerted Effort Needed to Consolidate and Secure Internet Connections at Federal Agencies http://www.gao.gov/products/GAO-10-237	April 12, 2010	40	To reduce the threat to federal systems and operations posed by cyber attacks on the United States, OMB launched, in November 2007, the Trusted Internet Connections (TIC) initiative, and later, in 2008, the Department of Homeland Security's (DHS's) National Cybersecurity Protection System (NCPS), operationally known as Einstein, which became mandatory for federal agencies as part of TIC. In order to further ensure that federal agencies have adequate, sufficient, and timely information to successfully meet the goals and objectives of the TIC and Einstein programs, the Secretary of Homeland Security should, to better understand whether Einstein alerts are valid, develop additional performance measures that indicate how agencies respond to alerts.
Cybersecurity: Progress Made But Challenges Remain in Defining and Coordinating the Comprehensive National Initiative http://www.gao.gov/products/GAO-10-338	March 5, 2010	64	To address strategic challenges in areas that are not the subject of existing projects within CNCI but remain key to achieving the initiative's overall goal of securing federal information systems, the Director of OMB should continue development of a strategic approach to identity management and authentication, linked to HSPD-12 implementation, as initially described in the Chief Information Officers Council's plan for implementing federal identity, credential, and access management, so as to provide greater assurance that only authorized individuals and entities can gain access to federal information systems.
Continued Efforts Are Needed to Protect Information Systems from Evolving Threats http://www.gao.gov/products/GAO-10-230t	November 17, 2009	24	GAO has identified weaknesses in all major categories of information security controls at federal agencies. For example, in fiscal year 2008, weaknesses were reported in such controls at 23 of 24 major agencies. Specifically, agencies did not consistently authenticate users to prevent unauthorized access to systems; apply encryption to protect sensitive data; and log, audit, and monitor security-relevant events, among other actions.
Efforts to Improve Information sharing Need to Be Strengthened http://www.gao.gov/products/GAO-03-760	August 27, 2003	59	Information on threats, methods, and techniques of terrorists is not routinely shared; and the information that is shared is not perceived as timely, accurate, or relevant.

Source: GAO.

Note: Highlights compiled by CRS from the reports.

Table 13. Selected Government Reports: White House/Office of Management and Budget

Title	Date	Pages	Notes
Trustworthy Cyberspace: Strategic Plan for the Federal Cybersecurity Research and Development Program http://www.whitehouse.gov/sites/default/files/microsites/ostp/fed_cybersecurity_rd_strategic_plan_2011.pdf	December 6, 2011	36	As a research and development strategy, this plan defines four strategic thrusts: Inducing Change; Developing Scientific Foundations; Maximizing Research Impact; and Accelerating Transition to Practice.
Structural Reforms to Improve the Security of Classified Networks and the Responsible Sharing and Safeguarding of Classified Information http://www.whitehouse.gov/the-press-office/2011/10/07/executive-order-structural-reforms-improve-security-classified-networks-	October 7, 2011	N/A	President Obama signed an executive order outlining data security measures and rules for government agencies to follow to prevent further data leaks by insiders. The order included the creation of a senior steering committee that will oversee the safeguarding and sharing of information.
FY 2012 Reporting Instructions for the Federal Information Security Management Act and Agency Privacy Management[a] http://www.whitehouse.gov/sites/default/files/omb/memoranda/2011/m11-33.pdf	September 14, 2011	29	Rather than enforcing a static, three-year reauthorization process, agencies are expected to conduct ongoing authorizations of information systems through the implementation of continuous monitoring programs. Continuous monitoring programs thus fulfill the three year security reauthorization requirement, so a separate re-authorization process is not necessary.
International Strategy for Cyberspace http://www.whitehouse.gov/sites/default/files/rss_viewer/international_strategy_for_cyberspace.pdf	May 16, 2011	30	The strategy marks the first time any administration has attempted to set forth in one document the U.S. government's vision for cyberspace, including goals for defense, diplomacy, and international development.
Cybersecurity Legislative Proposal (Fact Sheet) http://www.whitehouse.gov/the-press-office/2011/05/12/fact-sheet-cybersecurity-legislative-proposal	May 12, 2011	N/A	The Administration's proposal ensures the protection of individuals' privacy and civil liberties through a framework designed expressly to address the challenges of cybersecurity. The Administration's legislative proposal includes: Management, Personnel, Intrusion Prevention Systems, and Data Centers.
Federal Cloud Computing Strategy http://www.cio.gov/documents/Federal-Cloud-Computing-Strategy.pdf	February 13, 2011	43	The strategy outlines how the federal government can accelerate the safe, secure adoption of cloud computing, and provides agencies with a framework for migrating to the cloud. It also examines how agencies can address challenges related to the adoption of cloud computing, such as privacy, procurement, standards, and governance.
25 Point Implementation Plan to Reform Federal Information Technology Management http://www.cio.gov/documents/25-Point-Implementation-Plan-to-Reform-Federal%20IT.pdf	December 9, 2010	40	The plan's goals are to reduce the number of federally run data centers from 2,100 to approximately 1,300, rectify or cancel one-third of troubled IT projects, and require federal agencies to adopt a "cloud first" strategy in which they will move at least one system to a hosted environment within a year.

Title	Date	Pages	Notes
Clarifying Cybersecurity Responsibilities http://www.whitehouse.gov/sites/default/files/omb/assets/memoranda_2010/m10-28.pdf	July 6, 2010	39	This memorandum outlines and clarifies the respective responsibilities and activities of the Office of Management and Budget (OMB), the Cybersecurity Coordinator, and DHS, in particular with respect to the Federal Government's implementation of the Federal Information Security Management Act of 2002 (FISMA).
The National Strategy for Trusted Identities in Cyberspace: Creating Options for Enhanced Online Security and Privacy http://www.dhs.gov/xlibrary/assets/ns_tic.pdf	June 25, 2010	39	The NSTIC, which is in response to one of the near term action items in the President's Cyberspace Policy Review, calls for the creation of an on ine environment, or an Identity Ecosystem, where individuals and organizations can complete on ine transactions with confidence, trusting the identities of each other and the identities of the infrastructure where transaction occur.
Comprehensive National Cybersecurity Initiative (CNCI) http://www.whitehouse.gov/cybersecurity/comprehensive-national-cybersecurity-initiative	March 2, 2010	5	The CNCI estab ishes a multi-pronged approach the federal government is to take in identifying current and emerging cyber threats, shoring up current and future telecommunications and cyber vulnerabilities, and responding to or proactively addressing entities that wish to steal or manipulate protected data on secure federal systems.
Cyberspace Policy Review: Assuring a Trusted and Resilient Communications Infrastructure http://www.whitehouse.gov/assets/documents/Cyberspace_Policy_Review_final.pdf	May 29, 2009	76	The President directed a 60-day, comprehensive, "clean-slate" review to assess U.S. policies and structures for cybersecurity. The review team of government cybersecurity experts engaged and received input from a broad cross-section of industry, academia, the civil liberties and privacy communities, state governments, international partners, and the legislative and executive branches. This paper summarizes the review team's conclusions and out ines the beginning of the way forward toward a reliable, resilient, trustworthy digital infrastructure for the future.

Source: Highlights compiled by CRS from the White House reports.

a.   White House and Office of Management and Budget.

Table 14. Selected Government Reports: Department of Defense (DOD)

Title	Source	Date	Pages	Notes
DOD Information Security Program: Overview, Classification, and Declassification http://www.fas.org/sgp/othergov/dod/5200_01v1.pdf	DOD	February 16, 2012	84	Describes the DOD Information Security Program. and provides guidance for classification and declassification of DOD information that requires protection in the interest of the national security.
Defense Department Cyber Efforts: Definitions, Focal Point, and Methodology Needed for DOD to Develop Full-Spectrum Cyberspace Budget Estimates http://www.gao.gov/products/GAO-11-695R	General Accountability Office (GAO)	July 29, 2011	33	This letter discusses DOD's cyber and information assurance budget for fiscal year 2012 and future years defense spending. The objectives of this review were to (1) assess the extent to which DOD has prepared an overarching budget estimate for full-spectrum cyberspace operations across the department; and (2) identify the challenges DOD has faced in providing such estimates.
Legal Reviews of Weapons and Cyber Capabilities http://www.e-publishing.af.mil/shared/media/epubs/AFI51-402.pdf	Secretary of the Air Force	July 27, 2011	7	States the Air Force must subject cyber capabilities to legal review for compliance with the Law of Armed Conflict and other international and domestic laws. The Air Force judge advocate general must ensure that all cyber capabilities "being developed, bought, built, modified or otherwise acquired by the Air Force" must undergo legal review—except for cyber capabilities within a Special Access Program, which must undergo review by the Air Force general counsel.
Department of Defense Strategy for Operating in Cyberspace http://www.defense.gov/news/d20110714cyber.pdf	DOD	July 14, 2011	19	This is an unclassified summary of DOD's cyber-security strategy.
Cyber Operations Personnel Report (DOD) http://www.nsci-va.org/CyberReferenceLib/2011-04-Cyber%20Ops%20Personnel.pdf	DOD	April, 2011	84	This report focuses on FY2009 Department of Defense Cyber Operations personnel, with duties and responsibilities as defined in Section 934 of the Fiscal Year 2010 National Defense Authorization Act (NDAA). Appendix A - Cyber Operations-related Military Occupations Appendix B — Commercial Certifications Supporting the DOD Information Assurance Workforce Improvement Program Appendix C – Military Services Training and Development Appendix D - Geographic Location of National Centers of Academic Excellence in Information Assurance

Title	Source	Date	Pages	Notes
Critical Code: Software Producibility for Defense http://www.nap.edu/catalog.php?record_id=12979	National Research Council, Committee for Advancing Software-Intensive Systems Producibility	October 20, 2010	161	Assesses the nature of the national investment in software research and, in particular, considers ways to revitalize the knowledge base needed to design, produce, and employ software-intensive systems for tomorrow's defense needs.
Defending a New Domain http://www.foreignaffairs.com/articles/66552/william-j-lynn-iii/defending-a-new-domain	U.S. Deputy Secretary of Defense, William J. Lynn (Foreign Affairs)	September 2010	N/A	In 2008, the U.S. Department of Defense suffered a significant compromise of its classified military computer networks. It began when an infected flash drive was inserted into a U.S. military laptop at a base in the Middle East. This previously classified incident was the most significant breach of U.S. military computers ever, and served as an important wake-up call
The QDR in Perspective: Meeting America's National Security Needs In the 21st Century (QDR Final Report) http://www.usip.org/quadrennial-defense-review-independent-panel-/view-the-report	Quadrennial Defense Review	July 30, 2010	159	From the report: "The expanding cyber mission also needs to be examined. The Department of Defense should be prepared to assist civil authorities in defending cyberspace – beyond the Department's current role."
Cyberspace Operations: Air Force Doctrine Document 3-12 http://www.e-publishing.af.mil/shared/media/epubs/afdd3-12.pdf	U.S. Air Force	July 15, 2010	62	This Air Force Doctrine Document (AFDD) establishes doctrinal guidance for the employment of U.S. Air Force forces in, through, and from cyberspace. It is the keystone of Air Force operational-level doctrine for cyberspace operations.
DON (Department of the Navy) Cybersecurity/Information Assurance Workforce Management, Oversight and Compliance http://www.doncio.navy.mil/PolicyView.aspx?ID=1804	U.S. Navy	June 17, 2010	14	To establish policy and assign responsibilities for the administration of the Department of the Navy (DON) Cybersecurity (CS)/Information Assurance Workforce (IAWF) Management Oversight and Compliance Program.

Note: Highlights compiled by CRS from the reports.

Table 15. Selected Government Reports: National Strategy for Trusted Identities in Cyberspace (NSTIC)

Title	Source	Date	Pages	Notes
Recommendations for Establishing an Identity Ecosystem Governance Structure for the National Strategy for Trusted Identities in Cyberspace http://www.nist.gov/nstic/2012-nstic-governance-recs.pdf	NIST	February 17, 2012	51	NIST responds to comments received in response to the related Notice of Inquiry published in the *Federal Register* on June 14, 2011
Models for a Governance Structure for the National Strategy for Trusted Identities in Cyberspace http://www.nist.gov/nstic/2012-nstic-governance-recs.pdf	Department of Commerce	June 14, 2011	4	The department seeks public comment from all stakeholders, including the commercial, academic and civil society sectors, and consumer and privacy advocates on potential models, in the form of recommendations and key assumptions in the formation and structure of the steering group.
Administration Releases Strategy to Protect Online Consumers and Support Innovation and Fact Sheet on National Strategy for Trusted Identities in Cyberspace http://www.whitehouse.gov/the-press-office/2011/04/15/administration-releases-strategy-protect-online-consumers-and-support-in	White House	April 15, 2011	52	Press release on a proposal to administer the processes for policy and standards adoption for the Identity Ecosystem Framework in accordance with the National Strategy for Trusted Identities in Cyberspace (NSTIC).
National Strategy for Trusted Identities in Cyberspace http://www.whitehouse.gov/blog/2010/06/25/national-strategy-trust cyberspace	White House	April 15, 2011	52	The NSTIC aims to make online transactions more trustworthy, thereby giving businesses and consumers more confidence in conducting business online.

Note: Highlights compiled by CRS from the reports.

Table 16. Selected Reports: Cloud Computing

Title	Source	Date	Pages	Notes
A Global Reality: Governmental Access to Data in the Cloud - A Comparative Analysis of Ten International Jurisdictions http://www.hldataprotection.com/uploads/file/Hogan%20Lovells%20White%20Paper%20Government%20Access%20to%20Cloud%20Data%20Paper%20%281%29.pdf	Hogan Lovells	May 23, 2012	13	This White Paper compares the nature and extent of governmental access to data in the cloud in many jurisdictions around the world.
Cloud Computing Synopsis and Recommendations http://csrc.nist.gov/pub ications/nistpubs/800-146/sp800-146.pdf	NIST	May 2012	81	The National Institute of Standards and Technology has unveiled a guide that explains cloud technologies in "plain terms" to federal agencies and provides recommendations for IT decision makers.
Global Cloud Computing Scorecard a Blueprint for Economic Opportunity http://portal.bsa.org/cloudscorecard2012/	Business Software Al iance	February 2, 2012	24	This report notes that while many developed countries have adjusted their laws and regulations to address cloud computing, the wide differences in those rules make it difficult for companies to invest in the technology.
Concept of Operations: FedRAMP http://www.gsa.gov/graphics/staffoffices/FedRAMP_CONOPS.pdf	General Services Administratio n (GSA)	February 7, 2012	47	Implementation of FedRAMP will be in phases. This document describes all the services that will be available at initial operating capability—targeted for June 2012. The Concept of Operations will be updated as the program evolves toward sustained operations.
Federal Risk and Authorization Management Program (FedRAMP) http://www.gsa.gov/portal/category/102371	Federal CIO Council	January 4, 2012	N/A	The Federal Risk and Authorization Management Program or FedRAMP has been estab ished to provide a standard approach to Assessing and Authorizing (A&A) cloud computing services and products.

Title	Source	Date	Pages	Notes
Security Authorization of Information Systems in Cloud Computing Environments (FedRAMP) http://www.cio.gov/fedrampmemo.pdf	White House/Office of Management and Budget (OMB)	December 8, 2011	7	The Federal Risk and Authorization Management Program (FedRAMP) will now be required for all agencies purchasing storage, applications and other remote services from vendors. The Obama Administration has championed cloud computing as a means to save money and accelerate the government's adoption of new technologies.
U.S. Government Cloud Computing Technology Roadmap, Volume I, Release 1.0 (Draft). High-Priority Requirements to Further USG Agency Cloud Computing Adoption http://www.nist.gov/itl/cloud/upload/SP_500_293_volumeI-2.pdf	NIST	December 1, 2011	32	Volume I is aimed at interested parties who wish to gain a general understanding and overview of the background, purpose, context, work, results, and next steps of the U.S. Government Cloud Computing Technology Roadmap initiative.
U.S. Government Cloud Computing Technology Roadmap, Release 1.0 (Draft), Volume II Useful Information for Cloud Adopters http://www.nist.gov/itl/cloud/upload/SP_500_293_volumeII.pdf	NIST	December 1, 2011	85	Volume II is designed to be a technical reference for those actively working on strategic and tactical cloud computing initiatives, including, but not imited to, U.S. government cloud adopters. Volume II integrates and summarizes the work completed to date, and explains how these findings support the roadmap introduced in Volume I.
Information Security: Additional Guidance Needed to Address Cloud Computing Concerns http://www.gao.gov/products/GAO-12-130T	GAO	October 5, 2011	17	Twenty-two of 24 major federal agencies reported that they were either concerned or very concerned about the potential information security risks associated with cloud computing. GAO recommended that the NIST issue guidance specific to cloud computing security. NIST has issued multiple pub ications which address such guidance; however, one publication remains in draft, and is not to be finalized until the first quarter of fiscal year 2012.

Title	Source	Date	Pages	Notes
Cloud Computing Reference Architecture http://www.nist.gov/customcf/get_pdf.cfm?pub_id=909505	NIST	September 1, 2011	35	This "Special Publication," which is not an official U.S. government standard, is designed to provide guidance to specific communities of practitioners and researchers.
Guide to Cloud Computing for Policy Makers http://www.siia.net/index.php?option=com_docman&task=doc_download&gid=3040&Itemid=318	Software and Information Industry Association (SAII)	July 26, 2011	27	The SAII concludes "that there is no need for cloud-specific legislation or regulations to provide for the safe and rapid growth of cloud computing, and in fact, such actions could impede the great potential of cloud computing."
Federal Cloud Computing Strategy http://www.cio.gov/documents/Federal-Cloud-Computing-Strategy.pdf	White House	February 13, 2011	43	The strategy outlines how the federal government can accelerate the safe, secure adoption of cloud computing, and provides agencies with a framework for migrating to the cloud. It also examines how agencies can address challenges related to the adoption of cloud computing, such as privacy, procurement, standards, and governance

Notes: These reports analyze cybersecurity issues related to the federal government's adoption of cloud computing storage options. High ights compiled by CRS from the reports.

CRS Reports: Critical Infrastructure

- CRS Report RL30153, *Critical Infrastructures: Background, Policy, and Implementation*, by John D. Moteff

- CRS Report R41886, *The Smart Grid and Cybersecurity—Regulatory Policy and Issues*, by Richard J. Campbell

- CRS Report R42338, *Smart Meter Data: Privacy and Cybersecurity*, by Brandon J. Murrill, Edward C. Liu, and Richard M. Thompson II

- CRS Report RL33586, *The Federal Networking and Information Technology Research and Development Program: Background, Funding, and Activities*, by Patricia Moloney Figliola

- CRS Report 97-868, *Internet Domain Names: Background and Policy Issues*, by Lennard G. Kruger

- CRS Report R42351, *Internet Governance and the Domain Name System: Issues for Congress*, by Lennard G. Kruger

Table 17. Selected Reports: Critical Infrastructure

Title	Source	Date	Pages	Notes
ICS-CERT Incident Response Summary Report http://www.us-cert.gov/control_systems/pdf/ICS-CERT_Incident_Response_Summary_Report_09_11.pdf	U.S. Industrial Control System Cyber Emergency Response Team (ICS-CERT)	June 28, 2012	17	The number of reported cyberattacks on U.S. critical infrastructure increased sharply—from 9 incidents in 2009 to 198 in 2011; water sector-specific incidents, when added to the incidents that affected several sectors, accounted for more than half of the incidents; in more than half of the most serious cases, implementing best practices such as login imitation or properly configured firewall, would have deterred the attack, reduced the time it would have taken to detect an attack, and minimize its impact.
Energy Department Develops Tool with Industry to Help Utilities Strengthen Their Cybersecurity Capabilities http://energy.gov/articles/energy-department-develops-tool-industry-help-utilities-strengthen-their-cybersecurity	Department of Energy	June 28, 2012	N/A	The Cybersecurity Self-Evaluation Tool utilizes best practices that were developed for the Electricity Subsector Cybersecurity Capability Maturity Model Initiative, which involved a series of workshops with the private sector to draft a maturity model that can be used throughout the electric sector to better protect the grid.
Electricity Subsector Cybersecurity Risk Management Process http://energy.gov/oe/downloads/cybersecurity-risk-management-process-rmp-guideline-final-may-2012	Department of Energy, Office of Electricity Delivery & Energy Reliability	May 2012	96	The guideline describes a risk management process that is targeted to the specific needs of electricity sector organizations. The objective of the guideline is to build upon existing guidance and requirements to develop a flexible risk management process tuned to the diverse missions, equipment, and business needs of the electric power industry.
Cybersecurity for Energy Delivery Systems Program http://energy.gov/oe/technology-development/energy-delivery-systems-cybersecurity	Department of Energy, Office of Electricity Delivery & Energy Reliability	ongoing	N/A	The program assists the energy sector asset owners (electric, oil, and gas) by developing cybersecurity solutions for energy delivery systems through integrated planning and a focused research and development effort. CEDS co-funds projects with industry partners to make advances in cybersecurity capabilities for energy delivery systems.
ICT Applications for the Smart Grid: Opportunities and Policy Implications http://www.oecd-ilibrary.org/docserver/download/fulltext/5k9h2q8v9bln.pdf?expires=1330527950&id=id&accname=guest&checksum=F447004 3AC638BE19D5131C3D5CE5EA4	Organization for Economic Co-operation and Development (OECD)	January 10, 2012	44	This report discusses "smart" applications of information and communication technologies (ICTs) for more sustainable energy production, management and consumption. The report outlines policy implications for government ministries dealing with telecommunications regulation, ICT sector and innovation promotion, and consumer and competition issues.

Title	Source	Date	Pages	Notes
The Department's Management of the Smart Grid Investment Grant Program http://energy.gov/ig/downloads/departments-management-smart-grid-investment-grant-program-oas-ra-12-04	Department of Energy (DOE) Inspector General	January 1, 2012	21	According to the Inspector General, DOE's rush to award stimulus grants for projects under the next generation of the power grid, known as the Smart grid, resulted in some firms receiving funds without submitting complete plans for how to safeguard the grid from cyber attacks.
Critical Infrastructure Protection: Cybersecurity Guidance Is Available, but More Can Be Done to Promote Its Use http://www.gao.gov/products/GAO-12-92	General Accountability Office (GAO)	December 9, 2011	77	Given the plethora of guidance available, individual entities within the sectors may be challenged in identifying the guidance that is most applicable and effective in improving their security posture. Improved knowledge of the guidance that is available could help both federal and private sector decision makers better coordinate their efforts to protect critical cyber-re iant assets.
The Future of the Electric Grid http://web.mit.edu/mitei/research/studies/the-electric-grid-2011.shtml	Massachusetts Institute of Technology (MIT)	December 5, 2011	39	Chapter 1 provides an overview of the status of the grid, the challenges and opportunities it will face, and major recommendations. To facilitate selective reading, detailed descriptions of the contents of each section in Chapters 2–9 are provided in each chapter's introduction, and recommendations are collected and briefly discussed in each chapter's final section. (See: Chapter 9, Data Communications, Cybersecurity, and Information Privacy, pages 208-234).
FCC's Plan for Ensuring the Security of Telecommunications Networks ftp://ftp.fcc.gov/pub/Daily_Releases/Daily_Business/2011/db0610/DOC-307454A1.txt	Federal Communications Commission (FCC)	June 3, 2011	1	FCC Chairman Genachowski's response to letter from Rep. Anna Eshoo dated November 2, 2010, re: concerns about the implications of foreign-controlled telecommunications infrastructure companies providing equipment to the U.S. market.
Cyber Infrastructure Protection http://www.strategicstudiesinstitute.army.mil/pubs/display.cfm?pubid=1067	U.S. Army War College	May 9, 2011	324	Part I deals with strategy and policy issues related to cyber security and provides discussions covering the theory of cyberpower, Internet survivability, large scale data breaches, and the role of cyberpower in humanitarian assistance. Part 2 covers social and legal aspects of cyber infrastructure protection and discusses the attack dynamics of political and religiously motivated hackers. Part 3 discusses the technical aspects of cyber infrastructure protection including the resi ience of data centers, intrusion detection, and a strong emphasis on Internet protocol (IP) networks.

Title	Source	Date	Pages	Notes
In the Dark: Crucial Industries Confront Cyberattacks http://www.mcafee.com/us/resources/reports/rp-critical-infrastructure-protection.pdf	McAfee and Center for Strategic and International Studies (CSIS)	April 21, 2011	28	The study reveals an increase in cyber attacks on critical infrastructure such as power grids, oil, gas, and water; the study also shows that that many of the world's critical infrastructures lacked protection of their computer networks, and reveals the cost and impact of cyberattacks
Cybersecurity: Continued Attention Needed to Protect Our Nation's Critical Infrastructure and Federal Information Systems http://www.gao.gov/products/GAO-11-463T	General Accountability Office (GAO)	March 16, 2011	16	According to GAO, executive branch agencies have also made progress instituting several government-wide initiatives that are aimed at bolstering aspects of federal cybersecurity, such as reducing the number of federal access points to the Internet, establishing security configurations for desktop computers, and enhancing situational awareness of cyber events. Despite these efforts, the federal government continues to face significant challenges in protecting the nation's cyber-reliant critical infrastructure and federal information systems.
Federal Energy Regulatory Commission's Monitoring of Power Grid Cyber Security http://www.wired.com/images_blogs/threatlevel/2011/02/DoE-IG-Report-on-Grid-Security.pdf	North American Electric Reliability Corp. (NERC)	January 26, 2011	30	NERC developed Critical Infrastructure Protection (CIP) cyber security reliability standards which were approved by the FERC in January 2008. Although the Commission had taken steps to ensure CIP cyber security standards were developed and approved, NERC's testing revealed that such standards did not always include controls commonly recommended for protecting critical information systems. In addition, the CIP standards implementation approach and schedule approved by the Commission were not adequate to ensure that systems-related risks to the nation's power grid were mitigated or addressed in a timely manner.
Electricity Grid Modernization: Progress Being Made on Cybersecurity Guidelines, but Key Challenges Remain to be Addressed http://www.gao.gov/products/GAO-11-117	General Accountability Office (GAO)	January 12, 2011	50	To reduce the risk that NIST's smart grid cybersecurity guidelines will not be as effective as intended, the Secretary of Commerce should direct the Director of NIST to finalize the agency's plan for updating and maintaining the cybersecurity guidelines, including ensuring it incorporates (1) missing key elements identified in this report, and (2) specific milestones for when efforts are to be completed. Also, as a part of finalizing the plan, the Secretary of Commerce should direct the Director of NIST should assess whether any cybersecurity challenges identified in this report should be addressed in the guidelines.

Title	Source	Date	Pages	Notes
Partnership for Cybersecurity Innovation http://www.whitehouse.gov/blog/2010/12/06/partnership-cybersecurity-innovation	White House (Office of Science & Technology Policy)	December 6, 2010	4	The Obama Administration released a Memorandum of Understanding signed by the National Institute of Standards and Technology (NIST) of the Department of Commerce, the Science and Technology Directorate of the Department of Homeland Security (DHS/S&T), and the Financial Services Sector Coordinating Council (FSSCC). The goal of the agreement is to speed the commercialization of cybersecurity research innovations that support the nation's critical infrastructures.
WIB Security Standard Released http://www.isssource.com/wib/	International Instrument Users Association (WIB)	November 10, 2010		The Netherlands-based International Instrument Users Association (WIB), an international organization that represents global manufacturers in the industrial automation industry, announced the second version of the Process Control Domain Security Requirements For Vendors document—the first international standard that outlines a set of specific requirements focusing on cyber security best practices for suppliers of industrial automation and control systems.
Information Security Management System for Microsoft Cloud Infrastructure http://cdn.globalfoundationservices.com/documents/InformationSecurityMangSysforMSCloudInfrastructure.pdf	Microsoft	November 2010	15	This study describes the standards Microsoft follows to address current and evolving cloud security threats. It also depicts the internal structures within Microsoft that handle cloud security and risk management issues.
NIST Finalizes Initial Set of Smart Grid Cyber Security Guidelines http://www.nist.gov/public_affairs/releases/nist-finalizes-initial-set-of-smart-grid-cyber-security-guidelines.cfm	National Institute of Standards and Technology (NIST)	September 2, 2010	N/A	NIST released a 3-volume set of recommendations on all things relevant to securing the Smart Grid. The guidelines address a variety of topics, including high-level security requirements, a risk assessment framework, an evaluation of privacy issues in residences and recommendations for protecting the evolving grid from attacks, malicious code, cascading errors, and other threats.
Critical Infrastructure Protection: Key Private and Public Cyber Expectations Need to Be Consistently Addressed http://www.gao.gov/products/GAO-10-628	General Accountability Office (GAO)	July 15, 2010	38	Private sector stakeholders reported that they expect their federal partners to provide usable, timely, and actionable cyber threat information and alerts; access to sensitive or classified information; a secure mechanism for sharing information; security clearances; and a single centralized government cybersecurity organization to coordinate government efforts. However, according to private sector stakeholders, federal partners are not consistently meeting these expectations.

Title	Source	Date	Pages	Notes
The future of cloud computing http://pewinternet.org/Reports/2010/The-future-of-cloud-computing.aspx	Pew Research Center's Internet & American Life Project	June 11, 2010	26	Technology experts and stakeholders say they expect they will "live mostly in the cloud" in 2020 and not on the desktop, working mostly through cyberspace-based applications accessed through networked devices.
The Reliability of Global Undersea Communications Cable Infrastructure (The ROGUCCI Report) http://www.ieee-rogucci.org/files/The%20ROGUCCI%20Report.pdf	IEEE/EastWest Institute	May 26, 2010	186	This study submits 12 major recommendations to the private sector, governments and other stakeholders—especially the financial sector—for the purpose of improving the reliability, robustness, resilience, and security of the world's undersea communications cable infrastructure.
NSTB Assessments Summary Report: Common Industrial Control System Cyber Security Weaknesses http://www.fas.org/sgp/eprint/nstb.pdf	Department of Energy, Idaho National Laboratory	May 1, 2010	123	Computer networks controlling the electric grid are plagued with security holes that could allow intruders to redirect power delivery and steal data. Many of the security vulnerabilities are strikingly basic and fixable problems.
Explore the reliability and resiliency of commercial broadband communications networks http://hraunfoss.fcc.gov/edocs_public/attachmatch/DOC-305618A1.doc	Federal Communications Commission (FCC)	April 21, 2010	N/A	The Federal Communications Commission launched an inquiry on the ability of existing broadband networks to withstand significant damage or severe overloads as a result of natural disasters, terrorist attacks, pandemics or other major public emergencies, as recommended in the National Broadband Plan.
Security Guidance for Critical Areas of Focus in Cloud Computing V2.1 http://www.cloudsecurityalliance.org/csaguide.pdf	Cloud Security Alliance	December 2009	76	"Through our focus on the central issues of cloud computing security, we have attempted to bring greater clarity to an otherwise complicated landscape, which is often filled with incomplete and oversimplified information. Our focus ... serves to bring context and specificity to the cloud computing security discussion: enabling us to go beyond gross generalizations to deliver more insightful and targeted recommendations."
21 Steps to Improve Cyber Security of SCADA Networks http://www.oe.netl.doe.gov/docs/prepare/21stepsbooklet.pdf	U.S. Department of Energy, Infrastructure Security and Energy Restoration	January 1, 2007	10	The President's Critical Infrastructure Protection Board and the Department of Energy have developed steps to help any organization improve the security of its SCADA networks. The steps are divided into two categories: specific actions to improve implementation, and actions to establish essential underlying management processes and policies.

Note: Highlights compiled by CRS from the reports.

CRS Reports: Cybercrime and National Security

- CRS Report 97-1025, *Cybercrime: An Overview of the Federal Computer Fraud and Abuse Statute and Related Federal Criminal Laws*, by Charles Doyle

- CRS Report 94-166, *Extraterritorial Application of American Criminal Law*, by Charles Doyle

- CRS Report 98-326, *Privacy: An Overview of Federal Statutes Governing Wiretapping and Electronic Eavesdropping*, by Gina Stevens and Charles Doyle

- CRS Report RL32706, *Spyware: Background and Policy Issues for Congress*, by Patricia Moloney Figliola

- CRS Report CRS Report R41975, *Illegal Internet Streaming of Copyrighted Content: Legislation in the 112th Congress*, by Brian T. Yeh

- CRS Report R42112, *Online Copyright Infringement and Counterfeiting: Legislation in the 112th Congress*, by Brian T. Yeh

- CRS Report R40599, *Identity Theft: Trends and Issues*, by Kristin M. Finklea

- CRS Report R41927, *The Interplay of Borders, Turf, Cyberspace, and Jurisdiction: Issues Confronting U.S. Law Enforcement*, by Kristin M. Finklea

- CRS Report RL34651, *Protection of Children Online: Federal and State Laws Addressing Cyberstalking, Cyberharassment, and Cyberbullying*, by Alison M. Smith

Table 18. Selected Reports: Cybercrime/Cyberwar

Title	Source	Date	Pages	Notes
The Impact of Cybercrime on Businesses http://www.checkpoint.com/products/downloads/whitepapers/ponemon-cybercrime-2012.pdf	Ponemon Institute	May 2012	21	The study found that targeted attacks on businesses cost enterprises an average of $214,000. The expenses are associated with forensic investigations, investments in technology, and brand recovery costs.
Proactive Po icy Measures by Internet Service Providers against Botnets http://www.oecd-ilibrary.org/proactive-policy-measures-by-internet-service	Organisation for Economic Co-operation and Development	May 7, 2012	25	This report analyzes initiatives in a number of countries through which end-users are notified by ISPs when their computer is identified as being compromised by malicious software and encouraged to take action to mitigate the problem.
Developing State Solutions to Business Identity Theft: Assistance, Prevention and Detection Efforts by Secretary of State Offices http://www.nass.org/index.php?option=com_docman&task=doc_download&gid=1257	National Association of Secretaries of State	January 2012	23	This white paper is the result of efforts by the 19-member NASS Business Identity Theft Task Force to develop policy guidelines and recommendations for state leaders dealing with identity fraud cases involving pub ic business records.
A Cyberworm that Knows No Boundaries http://www.rand.org/content/dam/rand/pubs/occasional_papers/2011/RAND_OP342.pdf	RAND	December 21, 2011	55	Stuxnet-ike worms pose a serious threat even to infrastructure and computer systems that are not connected to the Internet. However, defending against such attacks is an increasingly complex prospect.
Department of Defense Cyberspace Po icy Report : A Report to Congress Pursuant to the National Defense Authorization Act for Fiscal Year 2011, Section 934 http://www.defense.gov/home/features/2011/0411_cyberstrategy/docs/NDAA%20Section%20934%20Report_For%20webpage.pdf	DOD	November 15, 2011	14	From the report: "When warranted, we will respond to hostile attacks in cyberspace as we would to any other threat to our country. We reserve the right to use all necessary means - diplomatic, informational, military and economic - to defend our nation, our allies, our partners and our interests."
W32.Duqu: The Precursor to the Next Stuxnet http://www.symantec.com/connect/w32_duqu_precursor_next_stuxnet	Symantec	October 24, 2011	N/A	On October 14, 2011, a research lab with strong international connections alerted Symantec to a sample that appeared to be very similar to Stuxnet, the malware which wreaked havoc in Iran's nuclear centrifuge farms last summer. The lab named the threat "Duqu" because it creates files with the file name prefix "~DQ". The research lab provided Symantec with samples recovered from computer systems located in Europe, as well as a detailed report with their initial findings, including analysis comparing the threat to Stuxnet.

Title	Source	Date	Pages	Notes
Cyber War Will Not Take Place http://www.tandfonline.com/doi/abs/10.1080/01402390.2011.608939	Journal of Strategic Studies	October 5, 2011	29	The paper argues that cyber warfare has never taken place, is not currently taking place, and is unlikely to take place in the future.
Revealed: Operation Shady RAT: an Investigation Of Targeted Intrusions Into 70+ Global Companies, Governments, and Non-Profit Organizations During the Last 5 Years http://www.mcafee.com/us/resources/white-papers/wp-operation-shady-rat.pdf	McAfee	August 2, 2011	14	A cyber-espionage operation lasting many years penetrated 72 government and other organizations, most of them in the United States, and has copied everything from military secrets to industrial designs, according to technology security company McAfee. See page 4 for the types of compromised parties), page 5 for the geographic distribution of victim's country of origin, pages 7-9 for the types of victims, and pages 10-13 for the number of intrusions for 2007-2010.
A Four-Day Dive Into Stuxnet's Heart http://www.wired.com/threatlevel/2010/12/a-four-day-dive-into-stuxnets-heart/	Threat Level Blog (Wired)	December 27, 2010	N/A	From the article, "It is a mark of the extreme oddity of the Stuxnet computer worm that Microsoft's Windows vulnerability team learned of it first from an obscure Belarusian security company that even they had never heard of."
Did Stuxnet Take Out 1,000 Centrifuges at the Natanz Enrichment Plant? Preliminary Assessment http://isis-online.org/isis-reports/detail/did-stuxnet-take-out-1000-centrifuges-at-the-natanz-enrichment-plant/	Institute for Science and International Security	December 22, 2010	10	This report indicates that commands in the Stuxnet code intended to increase the frequency of devices targeted by the malware exactly match several frequencies at which rotors in centrifuges at Iran's Natanz enrichment plant are designed to operate optimally or are at risk of breaking down and flying apart.
The Role of Internet Service Providers in Botnet Mitigation: an Empirical Analysis Bases on Spam Data http://citeseerx.ist.psu.edu/viewdoc/download?doi=10.1.1.165.2211&rep=rep1&type=pdf	Organisation for Economic Co-operation and Development (OECD)	November 12, 2010	68	This working paper considers whether ISPs can be critical control points for botnet mitigation, how the number of infected machines varies across ISPs, and why.
Stuxnet Analysis http://www.enisa.europa.eu/media/press-releases/stuxnet-analysis	European Network and Information Security Agency	October 7, 2010	N/A	EU cybersecurity agency warns that the Stuxnet malware is a game changer for critical information infrastructure protection; PLC controllers of SCADA systems infected with the worm might be programmed to establish destructive over/under pressure conditions by running pumps at different frequencies.
Proceedings of a Workshop on Deterring Cyberattacks: Informing Strategies and Developing Options for U.S. Policy http://www.nap.edu/catalog.php?record_id=12997#description	National Research Council	October 5, 2010	400	At the request of the Office of the Director of National Intelligence, the National Research Council undertook a two-phase project aimed to foster a broad, multidisciplinary examination of strategies for deterring cyberattacks on the United States and of the possible utility of these strategies for the U.S. government.

Title	Source	Date	Pages	Notes
Untangling Attribution: Moving to Accountability in Cyberspace [Testimony] http://i.cfr.org/content/publications/attachments/Knake%20-Testimony%2007151 0.pdf	Council on Foreign Relations	July 15, 2010	14	Robert K. Knake's testimony before the House Committee on Science and Technology on the role of attack attribution in preventing cyber attacks and how attribution technologies can affect the anonymity and the privacy of Internet users.
Technology, Po icy, Law, and Ethics Regarding U.S. Acquisition and Use of Cyberattack Capabilities http://www.nap.edu/catalog.php?record_id=12651&utm_medium=etmail&utm_source=National%20Academies%20Press&utm_campaign=NAP+mail+eblast+10.27.09+-+Cyberattack+Preorder+sp&utm_content=Downloader&utm_term=#description	National Research Council	January 1, 2009	368	This report explores important characteristics of cyberattack. It describes the current international and domestic legal structure as it might apply to cyberattack, and considers analogies to other domains of conf ict to develop relevant insights.

Note: Highlights compiled by CRS from the reports.

Table 19. Selected Reports: International Efforts

Title	Source	Date	Pages	Notes
Five Years after Estonia's Cyber Attacks: Lessons Learned for NATO? http://www.ndc.nato.int/download/downloads.php?icode=334	NATO	May 2012	8	In April 2007 a series of cyber attacks targeted Estonian information systems and telecommunication networks ... Lasting twenty-two days, the attacks were directed at a range of servers (web, email, DNS) and routers.The 2007 attacks did not damage much of the Estonian information technology infrastructure ... However, the attacks were a true wake-up call for NATO, offering a practical demonstration that cyber attacks could now cripple an entire nation dependent on IT networks.
Cyber-security: The Vexed Question of Global Rules: An Independent Report on Cyber-Preparedness Around the World http://www.mcafee.com/us/resources/reports/rp-sda-cyber-security.pdf?cid=WBB048	McAfee	February 1, 2012	108	Forty-five percent of legislators and cybersecurity experts representing 27 countries think cybersecurity is just as important as border security. The authors surveyed 80 professionals from business, academia and government to gauge worldwide opinions of cybersecurity.

Title	Source	Date	Pages	Notes
Cyber Power Index http://www.cyberhub.com/CyberPowerIndex	Booz Allen Hamilton and the Economist Intelligence Unit	January 15, 2012	N/A	The index of developing countries' ability to withstand cyber attacks and build strong digital economies, rates the countries on their legal and regulatory frameworks; economic and social issues; technology infrastructure; and industry. The index puts the United States in the No. 2 spot, and the UK in No. 1.
Foreign Spies Stealing US Economic Secrets in Cyberspace http://www.ncix.gov/publications/reports/fecie_all/Foreign_Economic_Collection_2011.pdf	Office of the National Counterintelligence Executive	November 3, 2011	31	According to the report, espionage and theft through cyberspace are growing threats to the United States' security and economic prosperity, and the world's most persistent perpetrators happen to also be U.S. allies.
The UK Cyber Security Strategy: Protecting and promoting the UK in a digital world http://www.cabinetoffice.gov.uk/sites/default/files/resources/uk-cyber-security-strategy-final.pdf	Cabinet Office (United Kingdom)	November 2011	43	Chapter 1 describes the background to the growth of the networked world and the immense social and economic benefits it is unlocking. Chapter 2 describes these threats. The impacts are already being felt and will grow as our reliance on cyberspace grows. Chapter 3 sets out where we want to end up—with the government's vision for UK cyber security in 2015.
Cyber Dawn: Libya http://www.unveillance.com/wp-content/uploads/2011/05/Project_Cyber_Dawn_Public.pdf	Cyber Security Forum Initiative	May 9, 2011	70	Project Cyber Dawn: Libya uses open source material to provide an in-depth view of Libyan cyberwarfare capabilities and defenses.
China's Cyber Power and America's National Security http://www.dtic.mil/dtic/tr/fulltext/u2/a552990.pdf	U.S. Army War College, Strategy Research Project	March 24, 2011	86	This report examines the growth of Chinese cyber power; their known and demonstrated capabilities for offensive, defensive and exploitive computer network operations; China's national security objectives; and the possible application of Chinese cyber power in support of those objectives.
Worldwide Threat Assessment of the U.S. Intelligence Community (Testimony) http://www.dni.gov/testimonies/20110210_testimony_clapper.pdf	James Clapper, Director of National Intelligence	February 10, 2011	34	Provides an assessment of global threats: convergence, malware, the "Chinese" connection, foreign military capabilities in cyberspace, counterfeit computer hardware and intellectual property theft, and identity theft/finding vulnerable government operatives.

Title	Source	Date	Pages	Notes
Working Towards Rules for Governing Cyber Conflict: Rendering the Geneva and Hague Conventions in Cyberspace http://vialardi.org/nastrazzuro/pdf/US-Russia.pdf	EastWest Institute	February 3, 2011	60	[The authors] led the cyber and traditional security experts through a point-by-point analysis of the Geneva and Hague Conventions. Ultimately, the group made five immediate recommendations for Russian and U.S.-led joint assessments, each exploring how to apply a key convention principle to cyberspace.
The Reliability of Global Undersea Communications Cable Infrastructure (The Rogucci Report) http://www.ieee-rogucci.org/files/The%20ROGUCCI%20Report.pdf	IEEE/EastWest Institute	May 26, 2010	186	This study submits 12 major recommendations to the private sector, governments and other stakeholders—especially the financial sector—for the purpose of improving the reliability, robustness, resilience, and security of the world's undersea communications cable infrastructure.
ITU Toolkit for Cybercrime Legislation http://www.itu.int/ITU-D/cyb/cybersecurity/docs/itu-too kit-cybercrime-legislation.pdf	International Telecommunications Union	February 2010	N/A	This document aims to provide countries with sample legislative language and reference material that can assist in the establishment of harmonized cybercrime laws and procedural rules.

Note: Highlights compiled by CRS from the reports.

Table 20. Selected Reports: Education/Training/Workforce

Title	Source	Date	Pages	Notes
National Centers of Academic Excellence (CAE) in Cyber Operations Program http://www.nsa.gov/academia/nat_cae_cyber_ops/index.shtml	National Security Agency (NSA)	May 29 2012	N/A	The NSA has launched National Centers of Academic Excellence (CAE) in Cyber Operations Program; the program is intended to be a deeply technical, inter-disciplinary, higher education program grounded in the computer science (CS), computer engineering (CE), or electrical engineering (EE) disciplines, with extensive opportunities for hands-on applications via labs and exercises.
Cybersecurity Human Capital: Initiatives Need Better Planning and Coordination http://www.gao.gov/products/GAO-12-8	General Accountability Office (GAO)	November 29, 2011	86	To ensure that government-wide cybersecurity workforce initiatives are better coordinated and planned, and to better assist federal agencies in defining roles, responsibilities, skills, and competencies for their workforce, the Secretary of Commerce, Director of the Office of Management and Budget, Director of the Office of Personnel Management, and Secretary of Homeland Security should collaborate through the NICE initiative to develop and finalize detailed plans allowing agency accountability, measurement of progress, and determination of resources to accomplish agreed-upon activities.
NICE Cybersecurity Workforce Framework http://www.nist.gov/manuscript-pub ication-search.cfm?pub_id=909505	National Initiative for Cybersecurity Education (NICE)	November 21, 2011	35	The adoption of cloud computing into the Federal Government and its implementation depend upon a variety of technical and non-technical factors. A fundamental reference point, based on the NIST definition of cloud computing, is needed to describe an overall framework that can be used government-wide. This document presents the NIST Cloud Computing Reference Architecture (RA) and Taxonomy (Tax) that will accurately communicate the components and offerings of cloud computing.
2011 State of Cyberethics, Cybersafety and Cybersecurity Curriculum in the U.S. Survey http://www.staysafeonline.org/sites/default/files/resource_documents/2011%20National%20K-12%20Study%20Final_0.pdf	National Cyber Security Alliance and Microsoft	May 13, 2011	16	This year's survey further explores the perceptions and practices of U.S. teachers, school administrators and technology coordinators in regards to cyberethics, cybersafety, and cybersecurity education. This year's survey finds that young people still are not receiving adequate training and that teachers are ill-prepared to teach the subjects due, in large part, to lack of professional development.

Title	Source	Date	Pages	Notes
Cyber Operations Personnel Report (DOD) http://www.nsci-va.org/CyberReferenceLib/2011-04-Cyber%20Ops%20Personnel.pdf	Department of Defense	April 2011	84	This report is focused on FY09 Department of Defense Cyber Operations personnel, with duties and responsibilities as defined in Section 934 of the Fiscal Year (FY) 2010 National Defense Authorization Act (NDAA). Appendix A - Cyber Operations-related Military Occupations Appendix B – Commercial Certifications Supporting the DoD Information Assurance Workforce Improvement Program Appendix C – Military Services Training and Development Appendix D - Geographic Location of National Centers of Academic Excellence in Information Assurance
Design of the DETER Security Testbed http://www.isi.edu/deter/news/news.php?story=20	University of Southern California (USC) Information Sciences Institute, University of California Berkeley (UCB), McAfee Research	January 13, 2011	N/A	The Department of Homeland Security (DHS) will invest $16 million over the next five years to expand a cybersecurity testbed at the University of Southern California (USC). The Deterlab testbed provides an isolated 400-node mini-Internet, in which researchers can investigate malware and other security threats without danger of infecting the real Internet. It also supports classroom exercises in computer security for nearly 400 students at 10 universities and colleges.
The Power of People: Building an Integrated National Security Professional System for the 21st Century http://www.pnsr.org/data/images/pnsr_the_power_of_people_report.pdf	Project on National Security Reform (PNSR)	November 2010	326	This study was conducted in fulfillment of Section 1054 of the *National Defense Authorization Act for Fiscal Year 2010*, which required the commissioning of a study by "an appropriate independent, nonprofit organization, of a system for career development and management of interagency national security professionals."

Note: Highlights compiled by CRS from the reports.

Table 21. Selected Reports: Research & Development (R&D)

Title	Source	Date	Pages	Notes
Information Security Risk Taking http://www.nsf.gov/awardsearch/showAward.do?AwardNumber=1127185	National Science Foundation (NSF)	January 17, 2012	N/A	The NSF is funding research on giving organizations information-security risk ratings, similar to credit ratings for individuals
At the Forefront of Cyber Security Research http://www.livescience.com/15423-forefront-cyber-security-research-nsf-bts.html	NSF	August 11, 2011	N/A	TRUST is a university and industry consortium that examines cyber security issues related to health care, national infrastructures, law and other issues facing the general pub ic.
Designing A Digital Future: Federally Funded Research And Development In Networking And Information Technology http://www.whitehouse.gov/sites/default/files/microsites/ostp/pcast-nitrd-report-2010.pdf	White House	December 16, 2010	148	The President's Council of Advisors on Science and Technology (PCAST) has made several recommendations in a report about the state of the government's Networking and Information Technology Research and Development (NITRD) Program.
Partnership for Cybersecurity Innovation http://www.whitehouse.gov/blog/2010/12/06/partnership-cybersecurity-innovation	White House Office of Science and Technology Policy	December 6, 2010	10	The Obama Administration released a Memorandum of Understanding signed by the National Institute of Standards and Technology (NIST) of the Department of Commerce, the Science and Technology Directorate of the Department of Homeland Security (DHS/S&T), and the Financial Services Sector Coordinating Council (FSSCC). The goal of the agreement is to speed the commercialization of cybersecurity research innovations that support our nation's critical infrastructures.
Science of Cyber-Security http://www.fas.org/irp/agency/dod/jason/cyber.pdf	Mitre Corp (JASON Program Office)	November 2010	86	JASON was requested by DOD to examine the theory and practice of cyber-security, and evaluate whether there are underlying fundamental principles that would make it possible to adopt a more scientific approach, identify what is needed in creating a science of cyber-security, and recommend specific ways in which scientific methods can be app ied.
American Security Challenge http://www.americansecuritychallenge.com/	National Security Initiative	October 18, 2010	N/A	The objective of the Challenge is to increase the visibility of innovative technology and help the commercialization process so that such technology can reach either the public or commercial marketplace faster to protect our citizens and critical assets.

Note: Highlights compiled by CRS from the reports.

Related Resources: Other Websites

This section contains other cybersecurity resources, including U.S. government, international, news sources, and other associations and institutions.

Table 22. Related Resources: Congressional/Government

Name	Source	Notes
Congressional Cybersecurity Caucus http://housecybersecuritycaucus.langevin.house.gov/index.shtml	Led by Representatives Jim Langevin., and Mike McCaul.	Provides statistics, news on congressional cyberspace actions, and links to other informational websites.
Cybersecurity and Trustworthiness Projects and Reports http://sites.nationalacademies.org/CSTB/CSTB_059144	Computer Science and Telecommunications Board, National Academy of Sciences	A ist of independent and informed reports on cybersecurity and public policy.
Cybersecurity http://www.whitehouse.gov/cybersecurity	White House National Security Council	Links to White House policy statements, key documents, videos, and blog posts.
Cybersecurity Wiki http://cyber.law.harvard.edu/cybersecurity/Main_Page	Berkman Center for Internet & Society (Harvard University)	Provides a set of evolving resources on cybersecurity, broadly defined, and includes an annotated list of relevant articles and literature, which can be searched in a number of ways.
Office of Cybersecurity and Communications (CS&C) http://www.dhs.gov/xabout/structure/gc_1185202475883.shtm	U.S. Department of Homeland Security	As the sector-specific agency for the communications and information technology (IT) sectors, CS&C coordinates national level reporting that is consistent with the National Response Framework (NRF).
U.S. Cyber Command http://www.defense.gov/home/features/2010/0410_cybersec/	U.S. Department of Defense	Links to press releases, fact sheets, speeches, announcements, and videos.
U.S. Cyber-Consequences Unit http://www.usccu.us/	U.S. Cyber-Consequences Unit (US-CCU)	U.S.-CCU, a nonprofit 501c(3) research institute, provides assessments of the strategic and economic consequences of possible cyber-attacks and cyber-assisted physical attacks. It also investigates the likelihood of such attacks and examines the cost-effectiveness of possible counter-measures.

Note: Highlights compiled by CRS from the reports.

Table 23. Related Resources: International Organizations

Name	Source	Notes
Australian Internet Security Initiative http://www.acma.gov.au/WEB/STANDARD/pc=PC_310317	Austra ian Communications and Media Authority	The Australian Internet Security Initiative (AISI) is an antibotnet initiative that collects data on botnets in collaboration with Internet Service Providers (ISPs), and two industry codes of practice.
Cybercrime http://www.coe.int/t/DGHL/cooperation/economiccrime/cybercrime/default_en.asp	Council of Europe	Links to the Convention on Cybercrime treaty, standards, news, and related information.
Cybersecurity Gateway http://groups.itu.int/Default.aspx?alias=groups.itu.int/cybersecurity-gateway	International Telecommunications Union (ITU)	ITU's Global Cybersecurity Agenda (GCA) is the framework for international cooperation with the objective of building synergies and engaging all relevant stakeholders in our collective efforts to build a more secure and safer information society for all.
Cybercrime Legislation - Country Profiles http://www.coe.int/t/dg l/legalcooperation/economiccrime/cybercrime/Documents/CountryProfiles/default_en.asp	Council of Europe	These profiles have been prepared within the framework of the Council of Europe's Project on Cybercrime in view of sharing information on cybercrime legislation and assessing the current state of implementation of the Convention on Cybercrime under national legislation.
ENISA: Securing Europe's Information Society http://www.enisa.europa.eu/	European Network and Information Security Agency (ENISA)	ENISA inform businesses and citizens in the European Union on cybersecurity threats, vulnerabilities, and attacks. (Requires free registration to access.)
German Anti-Botnet Initiative http://www.oecd.org/dataoecd/42/50/45509383.pdf	Organisation for Economic Co-operation and Development (OECD) (English-language summary)	This is a private industry initiative which aims to ensure that customers whose personal computers have become part of a botnet without them being aware of it are informed by their Internet Service Providers about this situation and at the same time are given competent support in removing the malware.
International Cyber Security Protection Alliance (ICSPA) https://www.icspa.org/about-us/	International Cyber Security Protection Alliance (ICSPA)	A global not-for-profit organization that aims to channel funding, expertise, and help directly to law enforcement cyber crime units around the world.
NATO Cooperative Cyber Defence Centre of Excellence (CCD COE) http://www.ccdcoe.org/	North Atlantic Treaty Organization (NATO)	The Center is an international effort that currently includes Estonia, Latvia, Lithuania, Germany, Hungary, Italy, the Slovak Repub ic, and Spain as sponsoring nations, to enhance NATO's cyber defence capability.

Note: Highlights compiled by CRS from the reports.

Table 24. Related Resources: News

Name	Source
Computer Security (Cybersecurity)	*New York Times*
http://topics.nytimes.com/top/reference/timestopics/subjects/c/computer_security/index.html	
Cybersecurity	NextGov.com
http://topics.nextgov.com/cybersecurity	
Cyberwarfare and Cybersecurity	Benton Foundation
http://benton.org/taxonomy/term/1193	
Homeland Security	Congressional Quarterly (CQ)
http://homeland.cq.com/hs/news.do;jsessionid=20B0A2F676BA73C13DDC30A877479F46	
Cybersecurity	Homeland Security News Wire
http://www.homelandsecuritynewswire.com/topics/cybersecurity	

Table 25. Related Resources: Other Associations and Institutions

Name	Notes
Cybersecurity from the Center for Strategic & International Studies (CSIS) http://csis.org/category/topics/technology/cybersecurity	Links to experts, programs, publications, and multimedia. CSIS is a bipartisan, nonprofit organization whose affiliated scholars conduct research and analysis and develop policy initiatives that look to the future and anticipate change.
Cyberconf ict and Cybersecurity Initiative from the Council on Foreign Relations http://www.cfr.org/projects/world/cyberconflict-and-cybersecurity-initiative/pr1497	Focuses on the relationship between cyberwar and the existing laws of war and conf ict; how the United States should engage other states and international actors in pursuit of its interests in cyberspace; how the promotion of the free flow of information interacts with the pursuit of cybersecurity; and the private sector's role in defense, deterrence, and resi ience.
Federal Cyber Service from the Scholarship For Service (SFS) https://www.sfs.opm.gov/	Scholarship For Service (SFS) is designed to increase and strengthen the cadre of federal information assurance professionals that protect the government's critical information infrastructure. This program provides scholarships that fully fund the typical costs that students pay for books, tuition, and room and board while attending an approved institution of higher learning.
Institute for Information Infrastructure Protection (I3P) http://www.thei3p.org/	I3P is a consortium of leading universities, national laboratories and nonprofit institutions dedicated to strengthening the cyber infrastructure of the United States.
Internet Security Alliance (ISA) https://netforum.avectra.com/eWeb/StartPage.aspx?Site=ISA	ISAal iance is a nonprofit collaboration between the Electronic Industries Alliance (EIA), a federation of trade associations, and Carnegie Mellon University's CyLab.
National Association of State Chief Information Offices (NASCIO) http://www.nascio.org/advocacy/cybersecurity	NASCIO's cybersecurity awareness website. The Resource Guide provides examples of state awareness programs and initiatives.
National Board of Information Security Examiners (NBISE) http://www.nbise.org/certifications.php	The National Board of Information Security Examiners (NBISE) mission is to increase the security of information networks, computing systems, and industrial and mi itary technology by improving the potential and performance of the cyber security workforce.
National Initiative for Cybersecurity Education (NICE) http://csrc.nist.gov/nice/	NICE Attempts to forge a common set of definitions for the cybersecurity workforce.
National Security Cyberspace Institute (NSCI) http://www.nsci-va.org/whitepapers.htm	NSCI provides education, research and analysis services to government, industry, and academic clients aiming to increase cyberspace awareness, interest, knowledge, and/or capabi ities.
U.S. Cyber Challenge (USCC) http://www.uscyberchallenge.org/	USCC's goal is to find 10,000 of America's best and brightest to fill the ranks of cybersecurity professionals where their skills can be of the greatest value to the nation.

Source: Highlights compiled by CRS from the reports of related associations and institutions.

Author Contact Information

Rita Tehan
Information Research Specialist
rtehan@crs.loc.gov, 7-6739

Key Policy Staff

Area of Expertise	Name	Phone	E-mail
General Policy Issues	Eric A. Fischer	7-7071	efischer@crs.loc.gov
General Policy Issues	John Rol ins	7-5529	jrollins@crs.loc.gov
Critical Infrastructure	John D. Moteff	7-1435	jmoteff@crs.loc.gov
Critical Infrastructure	Richard J. Campbell	7-7905	rcampbell@crs.loc.gov
Critical Infrastructure	Patricia Maloney Figliola	7-2508	pfigliola@crs.loc.gov
Critical Infrastructure	Lennard Kruger	7-7070	lkruger@crs.loc.gov
Cybercrime	Charles Doyle	7-6968	cdoyle@crs.loc.gov
Cybercrime	Brian Yeh	7-5182	byeh@crs.loc.gov
Cybercrime	Kristin Finklea	7-6259	kfinklea@crs.loc.gov
Cybercrime	Gina Stevens	7-2581	gstevens@crs.loc.gov
National Security	John Rollins	7-5529	jrollins@crs.loc.gov
National Security	Catherine A. Theohary	7-0844	ctheohary@crs.loc.gov,
National Security	Paul Kerr	7-8693	pkeer@crs.loc.gov